◆THE◆

CAESARS PALACE®

SPORTS BOOK OF BETTING

◆◆◆

Also by Bert Randolph Sugar

Rain Delays

◆THE◆

CAESARS PALACE®

SPORTS
BOOK OF
BETTING

◆◆◆

BERT RANDOLPH SUGAR

ST. MARTIN'S PRESS
New York

Design by Janet Tingey

Library of Congress Cataloging-in-Publication Data
Sugar, Bert Randolph.
    The Caesars Palace sports book of betting / Bert Randolph Sugar.
        p. cm.
    "A Thomas Dunne book."
    ISBN 0-312-05058-5
    1. Sports betting—United States. I. Title. II. Title: Sports book of betting.
    GV717.S84   1991
    796'.0973—dc20   91-20976
                                                   CIP

        First Edition: April 1992
    10 9 8 7 6 5 4 3 2 1

To everyone who has ever bet as much as
a Coke or a nickel on a game.
And won.

◆

"If you bet on a horse, that's gambling.
If you bet you can make three spades, that's entertainment.
If you bet cotton will go up three points, that's business.
See the difference?"

—Blackie Sherrod, Dallas *Times-Herald*

◆ CONTENTS ◆

✦ FOREWORD ✦

The Olympiad Race and Sports Book at Caesars Palace in Las Vegas, Nevada, is imposing. Some sports aficionados liken it to a slice of Heaven.

Picture this, if you will: an ornate, high-ceilinged, 16,000-square-foot facility containing some thirty video screens—one nearly three stories tall—broadcasting as many as five or six sporting events simultaneously . . . more than sixty electronic panels lining the walls with approximately 1.5 million red, green, and yellow light-emitting diodes specifying odds and various betting selections available to the thousands of daily visitors.

Every weekend, especially during the football and basketball seasons, the Caesars Palace Book atmosphere is electric with sports fans jammed elbow-to-elbow. Super Bowl Sunday is like New Year's Eve and Labor Day Weekend rolled into one. But whether it be the NCAA Final Four, baseball's World Series, the Kentucky Derby, the Masters golf championship, Wimbledon tennis, the Stanley Cup playoffs, or simply regular season games, the Caesars Palace Olympiad Book is world renowned as the mecca of sports gaming.

Open for business 365 days a year, action here is continual.

There are "overs and unders" and a myriad of other so-called propositions for the sports betting connoisseur. Who will score the first field goal in the Super Bowl? Who will record the most strikeouts in the American League this season? Will Larry outscore Michael in the Celtics-Bulls game? In addition to bets on today's events, you can place wagers on competitions scheduled months ahead. Literally thousands of proposition bet alternatives are available to sports gamblers every year. Yet while this environment can be fun and exciting, it also can be intimidating. First-time visitors to Caesars Palace are often overwhelmed when entering this world, no matter how familiar they may already be with sports and gaming.

This is why the people at Caesars were very pleased when Bert Sugar came up with the idea for this book. Bert is one person who can provide clarity, humor, and solid information on almost any subject found on the sporting scene.

Bert has been a friend of Caesars for years. Whether he is dining in one of Caesars Palace's gourmet restaurants or sitting with hundreds of reporters at ringside during a world championship fight, you can always spot him. He is the one in the famous hat, puffing the long cigar and, more often than not, clad in trousers featuring a rainbow of colors. More importantly, Bert Sugar is an acknowledged sports expert. Under that ubiquitous hat is a treasure chest of information. He is the one that many grizzled sportswriting veterans turn to for that single piece of trivia that adds an extra touch of expertise to a news story or column. He is the one who often provides rich anecdotes that give on-air broadcasters an additional dose of credibility with millions of listeners.

Needless to say, Bert Sugar is an accomplished journalist—writer, editor, broadcaster, and author of dozens of books. We are honored that he chose Caesars Palace as the property on which to base this book. There is no one better qualified, we believe, to break through the seeming complexities of a giant race and sports book operation.

In these pages you will find fresh insight into the world of sports and gaming, information that not only should be useful but equally entertaining. As Bert would be the first to tell you, this book will not guarantee your success as a sports gambler. It is not intended to be a definitive guide to sports betting. But it should make you feel more comfortable in this unique corner of the gaming universe, even if the author himself has conceded: "I picked Japan to win World War II, but I had seven-and-a-half points."

Kidding aside, Bert Sugar's observations should provide information and tips that will make your visit to a race and sports book—especially at Caesars Palace—more enjoyable as well as less intimidating. You will better understand the fascinating world of odds and oddsmaking as well as the nuances of sports and trends. You will better understand why betting lines are what they are. At the very least, this book should provide a sports fan with many hours of reading enjoyment.

HENRY GLUCK
Chairman and Chief Executive Officer
Caesars World, Inc.

◆ INTRODUCTION ◆

What the general public knows about legal sports betting probably can be written on the back of a picture postcard of the Las Vegas strip with plenty of room left over for "Wish you were here. Love, Madge."

Consider the 1990 Fiesta Bowl. The Crimson Tide of Alabama, appearing in its 25th consecutive bowl game, faced lowly Louisville, which was making only the fourth post-season appearance in its history. Although they were nine-point underdogs, the Cardinals of Louisville did not seem to know it. They made mincemeat of both Alabama and the odds, winning 34–7. After the game, Louisville head coach Howard Schnellenberger commented, "The oddsmakers didn't do their homework." But, truth to tell, Howard, they did.

The bookmaker's aim is not to reflect the final result, but to balance his books by offering odds that will attract equal amounts of money on both sides. Had the oddsmakers declared them even (Pick-'em) or made Louisville the favorite, they would have been overwhelmed by Alabama money, which would have placed them in the uncomfortable position of backing one team against the other rather than merely booking bets. The fact, Coach, is that since the point balance favored Alabama, it was the betting public who thought so little of your team's chances, not the oddsmakers.

Schnellenberger's comment is typical of many who do not quite understand the world of legal sports betting. And he is not alone.

Anyone entering that singular patch of land and state of emotion known as Caesars Palace Race and Sports Book for the first time is confronted by a scene so bewildering and intimidating they may well think they have wandered into the Pentagon Briefing Room by mistake. For there, amid the giant television screens carrying horse races run thousands of miles away; basketball and hockey games vie for attention; odds flash by, changing on the fly, electronic lists light the dark corners. Tension fills the room—winners hoping to parlay a fortune, losers hoping to get even. It is a sports fan's—and a bettor's—dream. Minus 140, plus 125, 27½ on the over—all around lies information, the essential tool for the sports bettor. But to the uninitiated, it can be bewildering, as useless as anything this side of the Lithuanian phone book.

It is the rare soul who can walk in for the first time and, without pausing to clear his throat or straighten his tie, step right up to the window and place a bet. Sure, there are a few intrepid souls who will damn the torpedoes and charge full-speed ahead, preferring to brave the minefield rather than admit they don't know what " − 140" means. Others, more timid perhaps—or maybe just more intelligent—refrain from taking part altogether. But the majority of those who walk in for the first time cannot comprehend why the favorite is quoted at " −6," let alone fathom the money line. It goes downhill rapidly from there, but many become caught up in the excitement and plunge right in nevertheless.

I must confess that I was once one of those tens of thousands who experienced that peculiar sensation, a kind of glazing over of the eyes, when I first entered Caesars Sports Book. I was not totally green. Like most modern Americans, I was familiar with the point spread as expounded by sportscasters on TV: "The Packers are three-point favorites," or "Take the Jets and the points." And I understood odds; I knew what it meant when I read that Marvin Hagler was 2–1 over Sugar Ray Leonard. They lost me when they quoted "Hagler −200, Leonard +140," though.

Standing there with as much dignity as I could muster, I looked around for some help, some guidance, before stepping off into this mysterious world of pluses and minuses. My first impulse was to walk over to the tellers behind the windows and apologize profusely for not knowing what I was doing. My second was to find out more about what was going on so I could bet with confidence.

Where to look? I pondered, almost out loud. My fellow elbow rubbers, guarding their secrets more carefully than Ft. Knox hoards its gold, were not very helpful in providing me with insights.

There were the so-called "tip sheets" published by betting services—touts, if you will—that literally littered the floor. Since the beginning of time, when man placed his first wager on a friendly game of rockball, entire forests have been sacrificed to the proliferation of these daily doses of delusion, all "guaranteeing" winners. But here, I soon found, it was a case of "Buyer Beware!" These tip sheets contain some winners, no doubt, but enough to make the reader a winner? Doubtful.

The writers behind the Sports Book windows were unimpeachably courteous and helpful, but their time was limited and my questions were unlimited. After holding up the line for ten minutes and incurring the wrath of the punters behind me, I beat a hasty retreat, my tail firmly lodged between my legs. There was not adequate time for a crash course in betting etiquette.

Where else to turn? The literature on legal sports gambling is meager at best. The would-be bettor who takes the time to seek out the Gamblers Book Club will be amply rewarded. This modest establishment, tucked away in the middle of the Las Vegas urban sprawl a couple of miles from "The Strip," houses a collection of virtually everything ever written about gambling of all kinds, from slots to hoops. (They regularly publish a comprehensive catalog and any serious student of gaming would do well to be on their mailing list.) A quick perusal of their shelves, however, yielded no sign of a primer on betting in an establishment like Caesars.

And so it occurred to me: Why not a how-to book on legal sports gambling? Not a "how-to"-*win* book, but a book that demystifies the runic world of odds and provides a basic starter kit, a few breadcrumbs, if you will.

Now, I don't promise you shortcuts or guarantees. Indeed, there are no "locks." It's sort of like the lawyer who billed his client $1,000.10. "The ten cents," he explained, "was for looking up the law. The thousand dollars was for knowing where to look." When you have finished with this book, you should know where to look. The looking will be up to you.

One important essential to begin earning your way is a working knowledge of numbers. This does not mean higher mathematics; calculus and differential equations are not required, but you must be—or be prepared to become—comfortable manipulating numbers. (Almost everyone has some blind spot with numbers. Take the great short story writer O. Henry, for instance. In his classic "The Gift of the Magi," he opens with "One dollar and eighty-seven cents. That was all. And sixty cents of it was in pennies." It does not require an Albert Einstein to see that it is impossible to make up the sum of $1.87 if sixty cents of it is in pennies.) If you can count over ten without taking off your shoes, you qualify. If not, there is no need to read on.

Remember the first time you figured out that 27 outs on one side of a baseball scorecard equaled the total number of putouts by the opposing side? Or that a touchdown in football was worth six points and a field goal three? Or any one of another dozen or so sets of numbers that form the basis of sports and that look to outsiders like cabalistic scratchings? Well, numbers in sports gambling are that simple; they just take some getting used to. Take the matter of a football point spread, such as:

LOS ANGELES RAMS   − 6   Green Bay Packers

As school children we learn that plus is more and minus is less, so this can be confusing at first. Upon closer examination, we realize that the Rams are considered to be six points better than the Packers, so the Rams are favored. (In fact, as we pointed out in the case of the 1991 Fiesta Bowl, they are not really considered that much "better." This is an artificial figure used by the linemakers to stimulate betting on both sides of the issue.) We shall encounter this "minus" quality in other numbers where it will indicate superiority. The favorite is required to "give away" points, as in this case, or the bettor must "lay odds" to back the favorite, so start thinking positive when you see a negative. After you become familiar with the numbers of sports betting they will become instinctive, not requiring a specialized form of intelligence.

As important as numbers are, they are just a part of a larger universe of information. Information is the specie of the sports bettor's sphere. It ranges from numbers to the NFL injury reports to Nolan Ryan's ERA to the juicy tidbit contained from your wife's-brother-in-law-who-is-dating-Michael Jordan's-landlady's-girlfriend. Sound reliable? Probably not, but that is for you to decide. Because sports handicapping makes such great demands on the bettor, you must evaluate all available information—weighing, sifting, accepting, rejecting, until you have formed your opinion. It will not all be cut to the same pattern. Most teams play better at home than they do on the road, but some play much better than others. What is this pitcher's lifetime record at home against that team? The visitors won their last three games, but how do they do on artificial turf? Does this bimbo really know Michael Jordan? Effective evaluation comes only with experience.

The possession of essential information can give the bettor a big edge. My own favorite story dates back to 1960. I had just left New York City with 50 cents in my pocket, heading back to the University of Michigan. Limited as I was to non–toll roads, the journey promised to be long. After some time I took a pit stop in a small Pennsylvania town that shall remain nameless, for reasons that soon will become evident.

The going price for a draft beer in the local watering hole was then 25 cents. At that rate, I was good for about ten minutes. But a free hard-boiled egg came with it, so I considered it a two-course dinner.

Savoring this modest repast, I glanced around the bar at the locals enjoying their boilermakers and a fight on TV. A fight! Gene Fullmer was fighting Carmen Basilio for the world middleweight title! These two battlers had squared off the previous year, a fact that the denizens of the bar seemed unaware of. It had been a Pier Six brawl, with relentless punching and toe-to-toe exchanges. Fullmer had kayoed Basilio in 14 rounds, the first time he had ever been stopped. Fullmer figured to repeat. I mumbled this piece of information aloud to no one in particular and, to my amazement, found I was surrounded by Basilio fans. Again I ventured the opinion that Fullmer would win, a little louder this time. That did it. Several of them offered to bet that Basilio would, in the words of one ring announcer, "emerge victorious." Not stopping to consider the downside risk to a man with but a single quarter left to his name, I happily covered all of the action around the bar.

The fight proved to be pretty much as I had envisioned it: a replay of the first meeting, but with Basilio finished in 12 rounds this time. By now my elbow-bending companions had meekly accepted the inevitable, and, polite beyond indictment, they paid in full. Generous to a fault, I stood the house a couple of rounds of drinks, had a good dinner, and, with the remaining profits tucked safely away in my wallet, proceeded on down the road, happy in the knowledge that a little information, like good wine, travels very far indeed.

My story is really just about being in the right place at the right time—by dumb luck—but it also serves to illustrate the importance of information. He who possesses it and evaluates it properly holds the power of a winner. I possessed vital information and, as a lifelong boxing fan, I knew how to interpret it in its present context. I had stumbled on an "overlay," the elusive object of all handicapping, a situation in which the probability of something happening is greater than the price being offered. (Although we were betting at even odds, I figured Fullmer to be at least a 9–5 favorite.)

That is what handicapping is all about: the careful accumulation and evaluation of information in the hope of finding a favorable betting situation, an overlay. But this takes time and effort. It means working hard at the learning process and always doing your homework.

The Caesars Palace Sports Book of Betting will guide you through the process. My object is to increase your appreciation and enjoyment of *legal* sports betting. Please note the emphasis on the word *legal;* Caesars and its Las Vegas competitors are in the bookmaking business. They make a profit from it, but they do so by furnishing a pleasant environment for the bettor, by supplying him with up-to-date information and by providing a fair and competitive market for the betting public. In this open and comfortable atmosphere, sports betting can be an exciting and rewarding pastime. Betting with an illegal bookie can, as they say on cigarette packs, be dangerous to your health.

It is my intention to enhance your betting pleasure by offering some insight into the process and by steering you in the right direction for acquiring and evaluating information. We cannot guarantee that you will become a winner; that is up to you. This we can offer: when you are through with *The Caesars Palace Sports Book of Betting,* you should be ready to make your own selections with confidence.

Before beginning, I must mention a few who have given generously of their time and expertise in giving this unique book form and flight: Henry Gluck, Chairman of the Board and Chief Executive Officer of Caesars World, who has been unstinting in his encouragement, as has Caesars World Vice President of Communications, Jack Leone, who has always been there when I needed him; Lou D'Amico, Director, and Vinnie Magliulo, Assistant Director of the Caesars Palace Race and Sports Book, have both been cheerful and willing contributors of anecdotes and historical odds as well as fact-checkers; Tom Dunne, my editor at St. Martin's Press, has effectively worn several hats, as cheerleader, coach, and cattle prodder. And Mort Olshan, Arne Lang, Bobby Bryde, Vinny DeMarco, Ed Curd—and even Jerry Berliant—have been there for help, encouragement, and information at the drop of a hat—mine, of course. Special thanks go to Allen Barra and George Ignatin; this dynamic duo gave me the benefit of their original approach to handicapping. And finally, thanks to my friend and collaborator, Alec Mackenzie, who has supplied not only much of the original background work and research but also a shoulder to more than occasionally cry upon.

When one considers that this is a seminal—meaning the first book of its kind ever attempted—one can understand that my task was made all the more difficult by the fact that there were no other works to research. And, because the only "ism" any writer believes in is plagiar*ism*, I had to rely on my own wits and those of my contributors. It, therefore, made their contributions to this book and to the lore of legal sports betting all the more essential. In truth, it has been priceless, which is what they were paid for their help.

BERT RANDOLPH SUGAR
Chappaqua, New York
June 7, 1991

◆THE◆

CAESARS PALACE®

SPORTS
BOOK OF
BETTING

◆◆◆

ONE

THE SUPER BOWL:
Where the Action Is

There's no such thing as a sure thing . . . that's why
they call it gambling.
                    —Oscar Madison

◆ ◆ ◆

Joe Montana stepped in over center and called the signals. With
the snap he dropped back and quickly checked his receivers.
San Francisco 49er wide receiver Jerry Rice worked himself
loose over the middle and broke for the post. Montana pumped
once and let the ball go. Rice took the ball in stride, bounced
off two would-be tacklers, and pranced into the end zone with
the first touchdown of Super Bowl XXIV.

All around us, pandemonium erupted. Rice's touchdown with
10:06 left in the first quarter was greeted with screaming and
yelling, even cursing, and more back-slapping than you'd find
at a Shriners convention. Some of the onlookers started dancing
in the aisles, jumping up and down like crazed jitterbugs, while
others—Denver Bronco backers, no doubt—grimly kept their
seats. You could almost hear them demanding, "Deal!"

It was the first of many to come, rewarding those who had
bet on Rice to score first at odds of 7–2. With the extra point
San Francisco assumed a 7–0 lead. As the teams lined up for
the kickoff, a fan yelled, "Give Elway some room!" There was
laughter and cheering and booing, enough to drown out John
Madden, at least for the moment.

The ball arched downfield on the giant screen, and settled

1

into the orange-clad arms of the Denver return man, Darren Carrington. He cut upfield. Bronco backers, anxiously waving blue-and-orange balloons and pom-poms, cheered momentarily. But then, almost as if letting the air out of their balloons, they heaved a collective sigh as Carrington was knocked out of bounds at the 25-yard line. In front of us, a middle-aged man wearing a red-and-gold baseball cap smacked the top of his desk. "Ahllll right!" he said.

It was Super Bowl Sunday at Caesars Palace, the most riotous scene since the storming of the Bastille. Combine equal parts of New Year's Eve, Mardi Gras and the trading floor of the commodities exchange and you will have a faint inkling of what Super Bowl Sunday at Caesars is like. The Oympiad Race and Sports Book was jammed with revelers, standing room only. The aisles were five-deep, effecting an almost complete strangulation of movement. In the back, where the fringes of the sports betting area merge with the casino, people had climbed atop slot machines hoping for a better view. Security guards chased them away, but they just ran around the back and climbed aboard again. After awhile, the guards gave up.

Just before the kickoff, Sports Book Assistant Director Vinnie Magliulo was approached by a patron. The man had just made a substantial wager and couldn't find a place to sit down and root for his money. He offered Magliulo $200 to let him sit in his office and watch the game on his little black-and-white TV. Vinnie turned him down but ruefully admitted later, "If I had a bigger office, I could have cleaned up." It was *that* crowded.

All weekend long, a holiday atmosphere had pervaded the halls and corridors of Caesars as some 5,000 fans invaded the stately pleasure dome. It was well nigh impossible to turn a corner without running into a crowd of orange-and-blue sweaters or red-and-gold warm-ups. Breakfast bagels and bialys were shared with fans from Brooklyn and Boise. Even at the blackjack tables the game was the subject of conversation. (Brian, one of the dealers in the Olympic Casino, liked Denver plus the points a lot. The player in the first seat agreed. The guy next to him offered to cover both of their bets. The lady in the third seat said, "Hit me.")

It was like this all over Las Vegas on Super Bowl weekend. Out on the Strip, traffic was at a standstill. The local newspapers estimated that hotel occupancy was something in excess of 95 percent—this in a town whose chamber of commerce laid claim to 67,391 rooms, give or take a room or two. Lou D'Amico, director of the Caesars Palace Olympiad Race and Sports Book, says that year in and year out, this weekend is the biggest of the year. In his opinion, "Las Vegas has become as important a destination as the host city." He estimates that on this day of days, the Caesars Sports Book alone plays host to at least 5,000 whacked-out sports nuts.

And yet, while Super Bowl fever gripped Las Vegas, it was not the only game in town. Long before the scheduled 5:18 P.M. (EST) kickoff, many of the choicest seats in the Sports Book— the desks provided by Caesars on a first-come, first-served basis—had been claimed by the regulars, horseplayers all. Magically transported across four time zones, their first East Coast post time is at 9:30 in the morning and they remain in action at four or five tracks until the sun sinks in the Pacific. They were all at their desks, figures at the ready, well before those who wager on two-legged studs had had their first cup of coffee.

Around the corner, in the annex added in 1989 to handle the growing crowds, basketball devotees were watching Duke vs. Georgia Tech. As the lead seesawed back and forth, they occasionally stole curious glances at the gathering Super Bowl throng. Otherwise, it was business as usual.

As the Sports Book began to fill up, the little knots of gamblers gathered, noisily sharing their wisdom with others. Eavesdroppers, giddy with anticipation, hovered on the fringes seeking confirmation of their betting beliefs.

Two of these groups formed around two legendary figures who, if there were a Hall of Fame for gamblers, would be among the first to be inducted. With their own money safely down, they were happy to share their wisdom with the Great Unwashed.

"Amarillo Slim" Preston had heard that a Reno sports book was offering an additional point over the prevailing Vegas line of Denver + 12½. (Situated in the northern part of the state, Reno and Tahoe tend to reflect betting patterns in neighboring northern California better than Las Vegas, which is often thought to be in Los Angeles's back yard.) Apparently believing John Elway when he said, "I guarantee we'll cover," Slim had sent a courier north in a small plane with several thousand in cash. This was on top of the substantial amount he had invested in Vegas. Like most professional gambling men, Slim is a shopper, always seeking a situation in which he senses that the odds offered by the books are out of line with his assessment of the outcome. As he reasoned before the game, the Broncos should have been eight- or nine-point underdogs. At 12½ to 13½, they were a great bargain. (Table 1.1 shows statistics for Super Bowl I through Super Bowl XXV.)

Lem Banker preferred San Francisco. Also a believer in getting value for his money, however, he had not backed it with his usual abandon, feeling that the price was too steep. Instead he had put his money into propositions.

At Super Bowl time—and always during major events in all sports—Caesars Sports Book offers an *à la carte* menu of "proposition" bets (see Table 1.2). For Super Bowl XXIV there were some seventy propositions in all shapes and sizes, including just about everything but the point spread on the "Bud Bowl." They ranged from 12–1 odds that the first touchdown would be scored on a punt or kickoff return to 30–1 that the total number of points scored would be 91 or more. "People love to bet props," says Vinnie Magliulo, whose fertile brain shapes them for Caesars. "We'll take anywhere from five-dollar to one-thousand-dollar wagers on them. It's like betting a game within a game."

TABLE 1.1: SUPER BOWL HISTORY

Super Bowl	Year	Site	Winner	Loser	Score	Spread	O/U	Half-Time Score
I	1967	Los Angeles	Green Bay (NFL)	Kansas City (AFL)	35–10, GBay	GBay –14		14–10, GBay
II	1968	Miami	Green Bay (NFL)	Oakland (AFL)	33–14, GBay	GBay –13		16–7, GBay
III	1969	Miami	New York Jets (AFL)	Baltimore (NFL)	16–7, N.Y.	Balt. –18		7–0, N.Y.
IV	1970	New Orleans	Kansas City (AFL)	Minnesota (NFL)	23–7, KCity	Minn. –12		16–0, KCity
V	1971	Miami	Baltimore (AFC)	Dallas (NFC)	16–13, Balt.	Dallas –2½		13–6, Dallas
VI	1972	New Orleans	Dallas (NFC)	Miami (AFC)	24–3, Dallas	Dallas –6		10–3, Dallas
VII	1973	Los Angeles	Miami (AFC)	Washington (NFC)	14–7, Miami	Wash. –1½		14–0, Miami
VIII	1974	Houston	Miami (AFC)	Minnesota (NFC)	24–7, Miami	Miami –6½		17–0, Miami
IX	1975	New Orleans	Pittsburgh (AFC)	Minnesota (NFC)	16–6, Pitt.	Minn. –3		2–0, Pitt.
X	1976	Miami	Pittsburgh (AFC)	Dallas (NFC)	21–17, Pitt.	Dallas –6½		10–7, Dallas
XI	1977	Pasadena	Oakland (AFC)	Minnesota (NFC)	32–14, Oak.	Oak. –4½		16–0, Oak.
XII	1978	New Orleans	Dallas (NFC)	Denver (AFC)	27–10, Dallas	Dallas –6½		13–0, Dallas
XIII	1979	Miami	Pittsburgh (AFC)	Dallas (NFC)	35–31, Pitt.	Pitt. –4		21–14, Pitt.
XIV	1980	Pasadena	Pittsburgh (AFC)	Los Angeles Rams (NFC)	31–19, Pitt.	Pitt. –11		13–10, L.A.
XV	1981	New Orleans	Oakland (AFC)	Philadelphia (NFC)	27–10, Oak.	Phil. –3		14–3, Oak.
XVI	1982	Pontiac	San Francisco (NFC)	Cincinnati (AFC)	26–21, S.F.	Cinc. –1	47	20–0, S.F.
XVII	1983	Pasadena	Washington (NFC)	Miami (AFC)	27–17, Wash.	Miami –3		17–10, Miami
XVIII	1984	Tampa	Los Angeles Raiders (AFC)	Washington (NFC)	38–9, L.A.	Wash. –3		21–3, L.A.
XIX	1985	Palo Alto	San Francisco (NFC)	Miami (AFC)	38–16, S.F.	S.F. –3		28–16, S.F.
XX	1986	New Orleans	Chicago (NFC)	New England (AFC)	46–10, Chic.	Chic. –10	38	23–3, Chic.
XXI	1987	Pasadena	New York Giants (NFC)	Denver (AFC)	39–20, N.Y.	N.Y. –8½	41½	10–9, Denver
XXII	1988	San Diego	Washington (NFC)	Denver (AFC)	42–10 Wash.	Denver –3	47	35–10, Wash.
XXIII	1989	Miami	San Francisco (NFC)	Cincinnati (AFC)	20–16, S.F.	S.F. –7	45½	3–3
XXIV	1990	New Orleans	San Francisco (NFC)	Denver (AFC)	55–10, S.F.	S.F. –12½	48	27–3, S.F.
XXV	1991	Tampa	New York Giants (NFC)	Buffalo (AFC)	20–19, N.Y.	Buff. –6½	41	12–10, Buff.

Proposition bets—or "props" as they are known among the gambling fraternity—have been around at least since the early '70s, available on just about everything up to, but not quite including, the Academy Awards and when the latest Russian spacecraft would land. (And although Caesars *does* set odds on some of these esoteric happenings, they do not accept wagers on them. But, then again, there are just so many things that can be bet on—ask Lloyds of London.) One of the first on the Super Bowl was the "Totals" (Over/Under) posted for Super Bowl XVI between the San Francisco 49ers and the Cincinnati Bengals. San Francisco won, 26–21, matching the Over/Under point total of 47, a "push." Despite this inauspicious beginning, proposition betting thrived in the fertile soil of Caesars Sports Book. Totals betting proved to be so popular that it quickly became part of the regular menu for all sports betting. In the next seven Super Bowls, the "over" won five times and the "under" twice. For today's game, the over/under line was 48.

Perhaps the most famous "prop" ever posted for a Super Bowl at Caesars was the 15–1 proposition that William "the Refrigerator" Perry, the Chicago Bears' defensive lineman who occasionally masqueraded as a fullback, would run or just fall forward for a touchdown in Super Bowl XX. "The Fridge," who had scored three touchdowns during the 1985 regular season—two rushing and one receiving—rewarded his supporters by scoring the Bears' fifth and final touchdown on a one-yard plunge in their 46–10 romp over the New England Patriots, costing Caesars a bundle.

That same Super Bowl also had planted the seed for yet another "prop" in the mind of Sports Book Director D'Amico. With four minutes remaining and the game on ice, Bears defensive tackle Henry Waechter tackled Patriots quarterback Steve Grogan behind the goal line for a safety. This was only the third safety in Super Bowl history.

Relying on his sense of history and an unerring instinct for the right odds, D'Amico posted a new prop for Super Bowl XXI between the New York Giants and the Broncos: Caesars laid odds of 4–1 that there would be no safety. All D'Amico can remember about the moment when Giants defensive end Leonard Marshall sacked John Elway was holding his head in his hands and wondering the extent of Caesars loss. It was a lot.

Hidden away among the 70 "props" on the electronic board for Super Bowl XXIV (see Table 1.2), Lem Banker saw one that looked as good to him as a $25 steak with mushrooms on the side. Caesars was offering odds of 11–2 (meaning that you had to lay $550 to win $100) that there would *not* be a missed extra point. An avid student of football statistics, Banker had calculated the chances of a professional placekicker missing a conversion at about one in eight, indicating that this bet was an overlay, that rare situation when the price offered on a given proposition is better than the probability of its coming to pass.

Other propositions had caught our eyes as well, particularly the one offering odds on the shortest field goal. My co-conspirator, Alec Mackenzie, and I figured that Denver would be so damned glad to get anywhere near the goal line on one of its early drives that they'd willingly settle for a three-pointer from in close. We took the +110 odds.

The Book also was offering parlay cards on the propositions and we combined bets that there would be more than three field goals, and fewer than 3½ sacks and that at least 13 points would be scored in the first quarter.

Throwing in one last wager on the over, we were ready to settle down and watch the game. That is, we were as ready as anyone can be to settle down, wedged in as we were, somewhere in the back near the slot machines, under a protective cover of orange-and-blue balloons.

TABLE 1.2: SUPER BOWL PROPOSITIONS
Super Bowl XXIV
San Francisco 49ers vs. Denver Broncos

Game Line: San Francisco −12
Money Line: San Francisco −700; Denver +500
Points: over/under 48

TABLE 1.2 *(cont.)*

Coin Toss: San Francisco or Denver −110
First Score of Game:
  First score is a touchdown −170
  First score is not a touchdown +130
First Touchdown of Game (by either team):
  Passing 3/5
  Rushing even
  Fumble or interception return 20/1
  Other (blocked punt or field goal return) 25/1
First Team to Score:
  49ers −190
  Broncos +150
Longest Touchdown Scoring Play:
  49ers −170
  Broncos +130
Player to Score First Touchdown:
  Jerry Rice (49ers) 7/2
  John Taylor (49ers) 4/1
  Roger Craig (49ers) 5/1
  Vance Johnson (Broncos) 6/1
  Ricky Nattiel (Broncos) 8/1
  Sammy Winder (Broncos) 10/1
  Tom Rathman (49ers) 10/1
  John Elway (Broncos) 10/1
  Brent Jones (49ers) 12/1
  Joe Montana (49ers) 12/1
  Steve Sewell (Broncos) 15/1
  Field (all others) 5/1
Team to Make First Field Goal:
  49ers −150
  Broncos +110
Team to Make Shortest Field Goal:
  49ers −150
  Broncos +110
Team to Make Most Field Goals:
  49ers −140
  Broncos even
Total Field Goals:
  Over 2.5 −220
  Under 2.5 +180
Most Touchdown Passes:
  Joe Montana (−½) −180
  John Elway (+½) +140
Total Receptions by Jerry Rice:

TABLE 1.2 (cont.)

Over 5½ −170
Under 5½ +130
There Will Be a Safety: +600
There Will Not Be a Safety: −900
There Will Be a Missed Extra Point: +300
There Will Not Be a Missed Extra Point: −500
Total Interceptions:
  Over 2.5 +110
  Under 2.5 −150
Total Quarterback Sacks:
  Over 3.5 −140
  Under 3.5 even
Most Pass Receptions (by):
  Jerry Rice −140
  Vance Johnson even
Super Bowl Shutout:
  49ers are shut out 40/1
  Broncos are shut out 15/1
49ers Will Win Game 7−0: 200/1
Broncos Will Win Game 5−0: 5000/1
Total Yards Rushing and Receiving by Roger Craig:
  Over 117 −120
  Under 117 −120
There Will Be Overtime: +800
There Will Not Be Overtime: −1200
Most Quarterback Sacks Made by:
  49ers −120
  Broncos −120
Scoring Will Occur by Either (or Both) Team(s) in Last 2 Minutes of
  First Half: −220
Scoring Will Not Occur in Last 2 Minutes of First Half: +180
Team to Score Last in First Half:
  49ers −190
  Broncos +150
The Last Score Will Be an Extra Point Conversion: −170
The Last Score Will Not Be an Extra Point Conversion: +130
Last Team to Score:
  49ers −180
  Broncos +140
Scoring by Quarters (Most Points):
  First quarter
    49ers −170
    Broncos +130
  Second quarter

TABLE 1.2 (*cont.*)

    49ers −250
    Broncos +200
Third quarter
    49ers −180
    Broncos +140
Fourth quarter
    49ers −200
    Broncos +160
Scoring by Quarters (Point Total, Both Teams):
  First quarter
    Over 7½ points −150
    Under 7½ points +110
  Second quarter
    Over 14 points −130
    Under 14 points −110
  Third quarter
    Over 10 points −130
    Under 10 points −110
  Fourth quarter
    Over 13 points −130
    Under 13 points −110
Total Points Scored in Game by Both Teams:
    0–10 30/1
    11–20 15/1
    21–30 6/1
    31–40 2/1
    41–50 even
    51–60 2/1
    61–70 6/1
    71–80 15/1
    81–90 30/1
    91 and up 30/1

Up on the big screen—the largest in the state of Nevada—
the Broncos' second drive stalled. They had to settle for a 42-
yard field goal by David Treadwell. This was good news: we
had bet that Denver would kick the first field goal on the parlay
card, and the 10 points scored put us well on the way to the
13+ points we had bet would be scored in the first quarter.
With 6:47 left in the first quarter, this last bet was looking good;
neither Elway nor Montana had been sacked and field goal num-

ber one had just gone down. We were a couple of real smart guys.

The complexion of the game soon changed, taking on a distinct red-and-gold hue as the San Francisco offense left the Broncos standing around like a bunch of retired saddle horses. It was rapidly becoming a blowout, the kind of game it is fun to watch only if you're a Niner fan. To Bronco backers it must have been excruciatingly painful. To the casual fan it had to be boring.

To most of the fans gathered in Caesars Sports Book, however, those of us who had bet the props, there were still a number of issues to be settled. Every time the 49er offense got down near the goal line we started hollering for them to go for the touchdown rather than the field goal, hoping that Treadwell's kick would hold up as the shortest, even though it had come from 42 yards. Time after time, the Niners obliged us, heading for the locker room at halftime in front by 27–3.

While Charles Schulz's "Peanuts" characters cavorted across the Louisiana SuperDome's artificial greensward at halftime, Caesars was staging its own festivities. They posted a halftime line offering San Francisco −5, meaning that the Niners had to outscore Denver by six points during the remainder of the game.

This, in effect—make that *in fact*—made it a whole new ballgame, and devotees of the point spread were out in force. San Francisco backers were loading up while Denver bettors were divided, some taking advantage of their last chance to "get even" before they headed home to wrap their wallets in laurel leaves and mourn their deceased bankrolls; others were taking the points in the vain hope that somehow John Elway still could make a football game out of it.

Like Lem Banker, we had liked the Niners, but not enough to lay 12½ points. Now, we were both believers. We had done our homework and knew that in 17 of the previous XXIII Super Bowls the team ahead at the half had won and 12 of them had won by a bigger margin than they had taken into the locker room. (See Table 1.3: Super Bowl Point Summary.)

But with all of our cash tied up in the props and the parlays, what were we going to bet with? Fortunately we ran into an old friend of unquestioned solvency. Pulling out a wad of bills the size of a football, he offered us as much as we liked, with some free advice: take San Francisco. That was good enough for us and we hied ourselves off to the windows.

The second half went pretty much like the first. In less than five ticks of the clock, the 49ers scored twice more—both touchdowns, thankfully—and led 41–3 with 9:44 left to play in the third quarter.

For Denver backers it was time for votive candles. They stood around offering excuses—like little boys trying to explain away their bad report cards—while San Francisco scored at will.

At the end of the third quarter, Elway ran it in from the three on a quarterback draw to close the gap slightly. On the drive, however, he had been sacked for the fourth time, losing us that bet and the parlay. But his touchdown accounted for the 50th point in the game, securing our bet on the over. When the 49ers' Tom Rathmann scored on the first play of the fourth quarter it had the effect of a three-alarm fire in an excelsior factory; it cleared the place out.

As Denver fans headed for the exits, their orange-and-blue balloons at half-mast, they seemed resigned to their fate. There was no talk of "next year." Over on the one side, we heard a

TABLE 1.3 SUPER BOWL I–XXV POINT SUMMARY

	Total Points by Quarters				
	1st Quarter	2nd Quarter	3rd Quarter	4th Quarter	Totals
Winning Team	125	217	160	168	670
Losing Team	67	80	56	110	313
Average Points Scored by Quarter (both teams)	7.7	11.9	8.6	11.1	39.3

Denver backer asking, "Know what the difference is between a flat and a blowout?" He hurried on to the punch line as if fearing he might be interrupted—or ignored: "When it's a flat," he said, "one Denver Bronco shows up. But when it's a blowout, the whole team shows."

There were other losers. It was general knowledge that Amarillo Slim had lost something in the neighborhood of $80,000 after shopping the whole of Nevada for value on the Broncos. Lem Banker had dropped a bundle when Michael Cofer, the San Francisco placekicker, pushed his second extra-point attempt wide to the right.

The next day, Slim defended his investment to us, saying he'd do it again. We didn't see Banker, but something about his bet had nagged us from the moment he had told us about it. Later on, it dawned on us: he had calculated his odds based on the *total number of extra points missed versus the total attempted.* His math worked out right and his reasoning would have been correct if that were indeed the proposition in question. Instead, what was at issue was whether or not an extra point would be missed in *this particular game.* We worked out the *percentage of games played in which there had been an extra point missed* and Caesars' odds were almost dead on; Banker had miscalculated, his bet was not an overlay after all.

There are a number of other lessons to be learned, which we shall consider later. For now, let's all take comfort in the fact that even the smartest and most successful gamblers don't win them all.

Super Bowl XXIV was history. The San Francisco 49ers had won big and the Denver Broncos had lost big. When we went to the windows to cash our bets, we, too, were winners in a modest way. (The field goal kicked by Denver's David Treadwell had been the only one made all day, so it qualified as both the shortest and the longest.)

In a very real sense, however, we were big winners, because there were no losers at Caesars that day—just non-winners. The fans at the SuperDome probably wouldn't want to admit it, but they had to have been bored to tears. The folks at home must have started flipping channels before Snoopy and Charlie Brown left the field at half time. Movie theaters around the country reported record attendance for the second half of a Super Bowl.

But, at Caesars there hadn't been a dull moment.

TABLE 1.4: ODDS TO WIN THE SUPER BOWL

Team	Opening Line* 1990	1991	1992
Minnesota Vikings	5	10	20
San Francisco 49ers	6	3	4
Buffalo Bills	6	18	4
Cincinnati Bengals	6	10	18
Los Angeles Rams	7	8	18
New York Giants	10	10	4
Chicago Bears	10	25	15
New Orleans Saints	10	15	30
Seattle Seahawks	12	40	30
Houston Oilers	12	20	14
Philadelphia Eagles	15	12	8
Washington Redskins	15	20	10
Cleveland Browns	15	15	200
Los Angeles Raiders	20	25	6
Denver Broncos	20	8	25
New England Patriots	20	45	300
Indianapolis Colts	35	40	50
New York Jets	40	100	100
Phoenix Cardinals	50	125	100
Miami Dolphins	50	25	15
Pittsburgh Steelers	75	22	18
Atlanta Falcons	80	80	75
Tampa Bay Buccaneers	100	60	75
San Diego Chargers	100	30	40
Kansas City Chiefs	100	20	12
Dallas Cowboys	100	125	40
Detroit Lions	200	35	30
Green Bay Packers	200	18	25

*Based on a $1.00 bet

TWO

FOOTBALL

FOOTBALL

On straight bets, player lays $11.00 for every $10.00 he wishes to win.

Example: The Raiders are a 3 point favorite. Player would
RAMS   lay $110.00 to win $100.00 or $550.00 to win
RAIDERS 3 $500.00, etc., on either team.

The point spread on the electronic display board is always by the favorite. If player wagers on the favorite, that team must win by more than the amount they are favored by. If player wagers on the underdog, that team can win the game or lose by any amount less than the point spread.

— On all straight bets (except Parlay Cards), if the favorite wins by the exact point spread, all money will be refunded.

— The home team is always listed on the bottom, unless specified otherwise.

Sunday, October 12, 1986 is an important date in recent history. In Reykjavík, Iceland, President Ronald Reagan met with Chairman Mikhail S. Gorbachev of the Soviet Union. The historic meeting signaled the beginning of the normalization of relations between the two world powers, the end of the Cold War.

Throughout the weekend the two world leaders had seen eye to eye on many matters. Sunday morning TV was filled with glowing reports of the rapport between the leaders and the progress in their arms reduction talks. But at the last moment, they agreed to disagree on one essential sticking point: the future of America's Strategic Defense Initiative, "Star Wars." This last-minute glitch was major late-breaking news.

Back home, the Dallas Cowboys were hosting the Washington Redskins in the second half of a TV doubleheader. It was a crucial game. The Cowboys, the defending NFC East champions, were "ahurtin'," as they say in Dallas: quarterback Danny White was out, running back Tony Dorsett and defensive stalwart Randy White were slowed by injuries, and the team was 3–2 for the first five games of the season. A victory over their division rivals was essential if they were to salvage the season.

With their backs to the wall, Dallas built a first-half lead based on the passing of backup quarterback Steve Pelluer and the running of USFL-refugee Herschel Walker. Failing to score in the third quarter, they took a shaky 16–6 lead into the final period. With the ball on the Redskins' 27, Pelluer faded back to pass. He spotted rookie wide receiver Mike Sherrard downfield, cocked his arm, and . . .

Without warning, CBS cut to Iceland.

In Las Vegas, the fans at Caesars Sports Book rioted. They screamed and hollered, threatening to tear the place apart. Wadded newspaper pelted the images of the world leaders on the giant screen. The air was filled with trash and bad language. As Sports Book manager Vinny Magliulo tells it, Caesars has no control over the TV feed; it simply displays the game, just like your corner tavern. But these hard-bitten bettors didn't know that. All they knew was the home 'dogs were ahead in a get-even game! Events taking place on a godforsaken island half a world away held no interest for them.

For the record, the Cowboys won the game, 30–6, and, at least as of this writing, the Cold War is still over. Perhaps Caesars should have posted a line on the Reykjavík summit; maybe Star Wars −6½.

Football betting—especially professional football betting—has become the single most popular gambling activity in America, not just at Caesars, but across the land. But it was not always thus.

Time was when baseball was the passion of the land. In saloon and salon alike, baseball was all the talk: Ty and Cy, Big Train and Big Six, Dizzy and Dazzy, and the Sultan of Swat. Football was as overlooked as Whistler's father, a game for college boys.

Baseball was the National Pastime—in fact as well as in name—for the first four decades of the twentieth century. And then, in what might be considered the most unlikely of places, Minneapolis, Minnesota, a singular development occurred that changed the course of betting history: Bill Hecht invented the point spread.

As a win-lose proposition, football is highly predictable. Even dominant baseball teams, like the Minnesota Twins, lose about four games out of every ten; but their football counterparts seem to roll on, week after week, making the oddsmaking business a dicey one. Before the point spread, bookies had a dilemma. If they set the odds at a level sufficient to attract a lot of business, they were liable to go broke; if they set them high enough to balance the books, they drove away customers. It was a two-edged sword, because picking winners was simply too easy. Football was not a betting sport because betting it was not a sporting proposition.

The point spread. It works like a golfer's handicap, allowing duffers to compete with scratch players. Where once there had been a sure thing, now there was room for a difference of opinion, which is the essence of gambling. It is the garlic in the salad, the one ingredient without which there is no dish. It is the great leveler, the device that brings true parity to the NFL. Unlike former NFL Commissioner Bert Bell's famous—if somewhat dubious—claim of parity, "On any given Sunday, any team in the NFL can beat any other team," the spread makes it happen, allowing pussycats to play powerhouses straight up. Because of it, sports betting was on the brink of a revolution.

The revolution got off to a rocky start, however. From around 1920 until the mid-thirties, Hecht's quoted double-numbered point spreads: "Yale is 13–15 over Harvard." This meant that if you liked the favorite, Yale, you had to give (or lay) 15 points; if you were a Harvard fan, you received 13 points. The number in between, 14, belonged to the bookie. With many contests landing right in the middle, this caused more than a little disgruntlement among the betting clientele. (See Table 2.1: The Spread vs. the Money Line in the NFL.)

Sometime around 1935, Bill Hecht resolved the difficulty with the two-number spread by quoting a single number. To eliminate the possibility of a push, he added a half-point as in "Yale − 13½ over Harvard." He offered 9/10 odds up to 14 points and 5/6 above it. He still quoted an odds line on the outcome, but with such outlandish prices as "1/20-15/1," there were few takers. Occasionally someone would take a flier on a longshot underdog, but few were foolish enough to lay 1/20 on the favorite in hopes of stealing a few easy bucks at the risk of losing the ranch.

TABLE 2.1: THE SPREAD VS. THE MONEY LINE IN THE NFL
(Money Line Conversions)

Point Spread	Money Line	
1	− 120	even
1½	− 130	+ 110
2	− 140	+ 120
2½	− 150	+ 130
3	− 160	+ 140
3½	− 170	+ 150
4	− 180	+ 160
4½	− 200	+ 170
5	− 200	+ 170
5½	− 200	+ 170
6	− 240	+ 200
6½	− 260	+ 220
7	− 300	+ 250
7½	− 350	+ 280

Although Hecht might have owned the original copyright, there was still room for improvement. The evolution of the point spread as we know it was finally completed in 1941 by Ed Curd of Lexington, Kentucky. Known in gambling legend as Frank Costello's bookmaker, Curd eliminated the outcome line and set the odds on the spread at 10/11, where it has remained to this day, guaranteeing the bookmaker a ten percent commission, or "vigorish"—on every bet booked.

But point spread or no, pro football had yet to reach the preeminence it enjoys today. It remained for the magic lantern of television to elevate it to its present exalted status. If it is possible to isolate a single magic moment when the romance between TV and the NFL began, it would come near the end of the 1958 season.

Playing in their next-to-last game of the season, the New York football Giants blocked a sure field goal attempt by Detroit's Jim Martin to preseve a 19–17 win. They were now one game back of the Eastern Conference leaders, the Cleveland Browns, with but one game to play. And that would be at home in Yankee Stadium, against these same Browns.

In that game, the Giants rallied to beat the Browns 13–10, and forced a playoff for the division championship. The following week, once again in Yankee Stadium, the Giants won the game 10–0, and with it the right to face the Western Division champion Baltimore Colts for the league championship.

It is important to note that until this time, New York had always been a baseball town, home to the Yankees, the Giants, and the Brooklyn Dodgers. But the previous year, both the Giants and the Dodgers had deserted their ancient ballparks to play in the greener ravines of California. Once baseball mad, now New Yorkers were just plain mad. Abandoned by the National League, they had no place to turn, for no *real* Giant or Dodger fan would be caught dead rooting for the Yankees. So little appeal had the Bronx Bombers locally that sportswriting's poet laureate, Red Smith, was once moved to write, "Cheering for the Yankees is like cheering for U.S. Steel."

With their heroics during this four-week period, the football Giants stepped forward to fill the void left by baseball. Overnight, they became the idols of a fandom starved for heroes. Lines formed nightly outside P.J. Clark's, the legendary Third Avenue bar known to be the players' favorite haunt. A glimpse of Frank Gifford or Charlie Conerly sent spinsters swooning; after an evening signing autographs, Kyle Rote had to seek shelter for fear that writer's cramp might threaten his ability to catch passes.

None of this, of course, was lost on the broadcasting and advertising types of Madison Avenue. They, too, spent their drinking time on Third Avenue. Fans themselves, they were quickly swept up in the hysteria that surrounded the Giants. And it showed. CBS, the network fortunate enough to be carrying the Giants-Colts championship game, ballyhooed it from morning till night; had there been commercial time available, it would have been snapped up in a moment. The game was already being billed as a clash of titans.

And that it was. Late in the fourth quarter, Steve Myra kicked a field goal for the Colts and regulation time ended in a 17–17 tie, thereby forcing football's first "sudden death" game. The Giants won the toss and elected to receive, but the Colts' stonewall defense forced them to punt. Under the steady hand of Johnny Unitas, the Colts worked the ball smartly down the field and fullback Alan Ameche dove over from the five to win, 23–17. The Giants had lost their first game in four weeks; but in so doing, they had played their way into sports history.

Pro football would never be the same again. Not just New York had watched "the Greatest Game Ever Played," the entire nation had. Pro football mania swept the land. After thirty-nine years it had finally arrived. Never again would it take a back seat to baseball or, for that matter, to college football.

Until this time, the NFL had conducted its business with television like a mom-and-pop store. Contracts were made on a market-to-market basis. Each franchise was free to sign the best deal it could in its area. But, like Orwell's pigs, not all markets were created equal. The New York market was suitably gigantic for the Giants, but tiny Green Bay was a tight squeeze for the Packers. Now, in the wake of the Greatest Game Ever Played, the young commissioner, Alvin "Pete" Rozelle, struck quickly. At the earliest opportunity, he pushed through a league-wide network TV contract with CBS. Henceforth the clubs would share the largess of network TV revenues equally.

Rozelle had a solid grasp of the power of television and how best to adapt it to the league's advantage. In the early years the league used the local-market blackout effectively as carrot and stick—it ensured full stadiums while the televised contests promoted the game. And unlike baseball, which was well suited to the one-dimensional medium of radio, pro football suffered at the hands of verbal interpreters; it needed the visual dimension television offered. The game's warlike character invited technological development; the isolated camera, the instant replay, slo-mo, freeze-frame, vivid statistical graphics—all were designed to boost production values and bring the fan closer to the field of action. Not incidentally, these developments enriched TV coverage of all sports.

Pro football and its newfound affiliates bulled their way into the sixties. Professional football now stood on the threshold of an unprecedented period of prosperity. But others wanted to be dealt in. Unable to gain admission to the NFL, a raffish band of entrepreneurs that included Al Davis and the outrageous Harry Wismer set up their own rump league, the American Football League. They held their own draft and procured their own television contract, guaranteeing survival. Thus armed, the new league dug deep into the pockets of well-heeled owners, such as Lamar Hunt and Barron Hilton, and declared checkbook war on the NFL. Sought-after college stars, like Billy Cannon, Bobby Bell, Johnny Robinson, Lance Alworth, and Otis Taylor quickly succumbed to the sweet smell of money. Then, in 1965, the AFL and New York Jets owner Sonny Werblin staggered the football world when he announced the signing of Alabama's outstanding quarterback, Joe Namath, for the unprecedented sum of $400,000.

This escalation was the beginning of the end. Al Davis soon took over as AFL commissioner and the league began signing active NFL quarterbacks, like the 49ers' John Brodie, to future contracts. This was the ultimate weapon. It was now evident that further warfare between the leagues would be economic suicide.

Peace finally came in 1966. With a single stroke, the NFL almost doubled in size, although the public had to wait until January 1967 for its first outward symbol. This was to be a game between the two league champions. The first edition of what would come to be dubbed the "Super Bowl" pitted Vince Lombardi's awesome Packers against Hank Stram's upstart Kansas City Chiefs. Las Vegas set the point spread at Packers 14 and—to no one's surprise—the Packers prevailed, 35–10.

Lombardi's charges repeated in 1968, beating the Oakland Raiders 33–14. It was generally felt that the AFL teams could not possibly reach parity with the older clubs before the merger was formalized in 1970; the NFL teams were just too strong. But Joe Willie Namath never paid more than lip service to tradition. As he led the upstart New York Jets to their Super Bowl III meeting with Don Shula's Baltimore Colts, predictions of their imminent demise were everywhere. They opened 18½-point underdogs, despite the fact that Broadway Joe "guaranteed" an outright win. Or so he told anyone who would listen, talk-show host or sportswriter or Miami barfly. No one paid much attention. In fact, no one seemed to care very much, as the Jets drifted lower against the spread, ending up as 17½-point dogs. But Namath was as good as his word. The Jets controlled the game throughout and won it 16–7, and with it, respect for their upstart league.

But the NFL was the big winner. In that moment, the Super Bowl became the single most watched, hyped, talked about, ballyhooed, *and bet-on* event in all of sports. It was the perfect offspring of the marriage of pro football and television.

◆ ◆ ◆

Pete Rozelle seldom opened a door without a strategy. He knew that the future of televised football lay in more exposure, not on Sunday afternoons, but in prime time. So he sought both less exposure and more exposure—less on Sundays, when doubleheaders depressed the ratings, and more on weeknights, when the games might attract an all-new audience, women.

He presented his plan first to CBS, the biggest spender for pro football rights. But Monday was the one-eyed network's most successful night of the week and top management was loathe to tamper with it. So Rozelle ambled down Sixth Avenue to see number two on his list of financial benefactors, NBC. But that network had recently purchased an expensive package of movies to counter CBS's Monday night domination, so they passed, too. Undaunted, the Commissioner turned to TV's step-children, ABC and the Hughes Sports Network.

It would not be uncharitable to characterize ABC-TV at this time as fourth in a three-horse race. The network was trying to rebound from a disastrous season, and management desperately sought any programming that looked like a lifesaver. So they were eager to talk to Rozelle. Hughes was, too; but they offered a network with very few stations, so ABC it was.

After protracted negotiations, they made a solid offer of $8.5 million a year for three years. For this they received thirteen "attractive" regular season games, which Rozelle neatly sliced out of the CBS and NBC packages.

Monday night would never be the same. Until "Monday Night Football" kicked off in 1970, the TV show that had packed the greatest sociological impact had been "The Texaco Star Thea-ter" with Milton Berle in the early fifties. Uncle Miltie was said to have sold more television sets than gasoline. But with the advent of football in prime time, restaurants closed, theater business fell off, doctors even refused to deliver babies until the final gun. The NFL received impassioned letters from wives who credited "Monday Night Football" with saving their marriages by keeping the old man at home. And, where Berle had merely lightened the burden of the workweek, Rozelle had succeeded in extending the weekend. How's that for cultural impact?

"Monday Night Football" was just the consummation of the love affair between pro football and the tube. The extension of that romance to betting is a natural one; we all love to watch our money in action. (See Table 2.2: Monday Night Won-Lost Records, 1986–1990.) Breathes there an investor, however small, who, upon purchasing a stock, did not rush right out to buy the evening paper to see how his acquisition did that day? And as Wall Street goes, so goes Las Vegas. In fact, the bigger the bettor, the better the spectator.

Although all NFL games—and, courtesy of cable, most major college games—are televised and, while full coverage is not available in every market, developments in all games are updated frequently, so the bettor can stay right on top of the action. Small wonder that Caesars sports the largest TV screen in the state of Nevada or that so many satellite dishes have sprouted up around Las Vegas that one wag has suggested that they should be named Nevada's state flower.

Despite the immense TV exposure, there are relatively few betting opportunities in pro football. With 28 teams playing 16 games, there are only 224 contests during the regular season. Compare this to baseball's 2,106 contests and it may seem like limited action. Actually, to the casual bettor, this can be a blessing. Beginning with the 1990 season, there are only 13 games a week, and all are played on the weekend or at night. This leaves plenty of time for handicapping and, for most, an opportunity to watch the game and root for your money.

The NFL has always tacitly acknowledged the gambling connection. As a result, it has always been forthcoming with information. By league rule, injuries must be reported early in the week so as not to provide an unintentional hidden advantage to gamblers or bookmakers. In the past, pregame shows have

Table 2.2: Monday Night Won-Lost Records, 1986–1990

AFC	Total	1990	1989	1988	1987	1986
Buffalo Bills	4–3	1–1	1–2	2–0		
Cincinnati Bengals	3–3	1–1	1–2			1–0
Cleveland Browns	5–4	1–1	1–1	1–2	1–0	1–0
Denver Broncos	6–5	1–1	2–0	0–2	2–1	1–1
Houston Oilers	3–0	1–0	1–0	1–0		
Indianapolis Colts	1–2	0–1		1–1		
Kansas City Chiefs	0–1	0–1				
L.A. Raiders	5–3	2–0	1–0	1–1	1–1	0–1
Miami Dolphins	3–5	0–1		1–1	1–1	1–2
New England Patriots	2–1				1–1	1–0
N.Y. Jets	3–5	0–1	0–1	0–1	2–1	1–1
Pittsburgh Steelers	1–2	1–0				0–2
San Diego Chargers	0–1					0–1
Seattle Seahawks	5–2	1–0	1–0	1–0	0–2	2–0
NFC						
Atlanta Falcons	0–0					
Chicago Bears	5–6		1–1	1–2	1–2	2–1
Dallas Cowboys	5–2			1–1	2–1	2–0
Detroit Lions	0–2	0–1				0–1
Green Bay Packers	0–1					0–1
L.A. Rams	3–7	0–3	0–2	1–0	1–2	1–0
Minnesota Vikings	3–2	0–1	1–1	1–0	1–0	
New Orleans Saints	3–2	1–1	1–1	1–0		
N.Y. Giants	6–7	1–1	2–1	1–1	0–3	2–1
Philadelphia Eagles	3–2	2–0	0–2	1–0		
Phoenix Cardinals	0–2			0–1		0–1
San Francisco 49ers	9–3	3–0	3–0	1–1	2–0	0–2
Tampa Bay Bucs	0–0					
Washington Redskins	2–7	0–1	0–2	0–2	1–1	1–1

Monday Night Syndrome
1990
Of the 15 winning teams on
   Monday Night Football:

        9 won the next week
        6 lost the next week
        0 tied the next week

Of the 15 losing teams on
   Monday Night Football:

        10 won the next week
        4 lost the next week
        0 tied the next week
        1 had an Open Date the next week

TABLE 2.2 (*cont.*)

Of all 30 teams on Monday Night Football:	
	19 won the next week
	10 lost the next week
	0 tied the next week
	1 had an Open Date the next week

spotlighted the point spreads—often offering selections—as have newspapers throughout the country. And, as in all big-time sports, statistical records abound, offering the bettor a wealth of information to analyze.

This is not entirely by accident; the NFL can trace much of its ancestry directly back to legalized gambling. In the twenties, when sports betting was legal in New York, the fledgling NFL eagerly offered its most promising franchise to Tim Mara for the piddling sum of $2,500. Mara, who ran what was perhaps the most successful—and certainly one of the most respected—bookmaking establishments of the time, graciously accepted, maintaining that "an exclusive franchise for anything in New York is worth $2,500." Mara's descendants retained full ownership of the Giants until early in 1991 when they sold 50 percent for a handsome sum in the neighborhood of $60–$70 million. Not a bad neighborhood for an investment of $2,500.

Another NFL pioneer who owed his franchise directly to gambling proceeds was Art Rooney, a man who, by his own admission, was "never afraid to bet." During one legendary string of racetrack wins, according to Red Smith, Rooney "slapped the bookmakers around for more than a quarter-million." It began at the old Empire City track in Yonkers, New York, and extended upstate to Saratoga. (Ironically, the thoroughbred operation eventually closed down at Empire State, which reemerged as a half-mile harness track called Yonkers Raceway, owned by the Rooney family.) Rooney used his winnings to buy into the NFL with a team this lovable swashbuckler appropriately called the Pirates. He later changed the name to the Steelers.

This was in 1933, the year Pennsylvania abolished its Blue Laws, thus allowing Sunday football. Joining Rooney as an NFL newcomer was fellow Pennsylvanian Bert Bell, who bought the Frankfort Yellowjackets and moved them to the city of Philadelphia where they became the Eagles.

Soon afterward, Bell received an appeal from the president of the American Totalizator Company, makers of racetrack parimutuel machines. He beseeched his old friend to help him get his son out of trouble. It seems that the son, then a student at the University of Pennsylvania, had gotten himself in difficulty gambling over his head. Whatever Bell did seemed to work, and eventually the son, Carroll Rosenbloom, was welcomed into the NFL as the owner of first the Baltimore Colts and later the Los Angeles Rams.

In the early fifties, Johnny Unitas, late of Louisville University and the Pittsburgh Steelers, was relegated to minor league football after the Steelers gave him his pink slip. He summarized his days as a semipro in one sentence: "They didn't have a team bus, they had a team bike." There was no money for equipment, no money for uniforms, no money for salaries. As Milton Berle relates, in *B.S. I Love You*, while Unitas filled in for the Bloomington Rams—awaiting the call from the Baltimore Colts that would bring him to stardom and eventual immortality—"Unitas was rewarded with six dollars a game, win or lose. Side bets brought in an extra ten." At those prices, a side bet was a necessity.

Thus the pillars of football, true to their heritage, have always been cordial to the betting world while keeping it at arm's length. Tacitly admitting that much of their sport's popularity stems from its appeal to the betting public, the NFL allowed— even encouraged—pregame TV prognosticators like Jimmy "the Greek" Snyder.

But then in 1990, the new commissioner, Paul Tagliabue, executed an audible, announcing a new policy regarding betting information. Perhaps prompted by the Oregon Lottery, which recently had adopted sports betting, Tagliabue viewed the public discussion of the point spread by his client TV networks with all the warmth the Romans once reserved for marauding Visigoths. No longer would television be allowed to discuss that threat to civil order, motherhood and the American flag, the point spread.

At this juncture, the net result of this move is not known. It may, perhaps, be sacrilegious to consider the alternative, but studies have shown that fully 30 percent of all viewers have a little something on the outcome—or they wouldn't be watching. And practically every major newspaper in the country at least publishes the line, with many going a great deal further, turning the media "into the football Racing Form," in the words of Harvey Araton of the New York *Daily News.* "The NFL doesn't sell its players," Araton continued, "and it doesn't hawk its stories as much as it sells its point spreads." To be continued. . . .

Week in and week out during the season, millions wrestle with the challenge of handicapping football, only to find that the point spread is indeed the great leveler it is intended to be. The gambler now finds himself—like the aforementioned baseball teams—fortunate to win even six out of every ten games. Indeed, when bucking the 10/11 odds, he must win at least 52.38 percent of his bets to break even, a task that is a good deal more difficult than it appears on the surface. One reason for this is the presence of random chance, a factor known to most bettors as luck.

All games can be separated into two categories: games of skill and games of chance. Although occasionally there may be a modest amount of skill associated with certain games of chance, it is small and has little influence on the outcome. Games of chance include all casino games—with the possible exception of blackjack, depending on your skill level—lotteries, and trying to hit the Pick Six at the racetrack.

Games of skill include poker, bridge, backgammon, chess and, of course, all of the sports under discussion here. Random chance, or luck, still plays a hand in these games as well—the luck of the draw, the roll of the dice or the bounce of a football. For this reason, these games retain a high degree of unpredictability. This varies from game to game and from contest to contest, depending, in part, on the skill levels of the participants. Casino players who are unfamiliar with blackjack strategy *will* lose; those who use it *may* win; card counters *will* win. The Minnesota Twins may currently be the best team in baseball, but they still will lose about 35 or 40 percent of the time. The best horse does not always win the race. The better football team usually *will* win the game, but even if they do, they may not cover the spread.

And therein lies the rub. The point spread has its effect, transforming a highly predictable result—the straight-up outcome in which luck plays a small role—into a highly *un*predictable one in which luck plays a large role. Because victory against the point spread can go either way, the element of luck becomes very important. How often have you had much the better team only to watch them win but still fail to cover?

The key to predicting the outcome of any contest is in eliminating the possibility of random chance present in every contest. This is, of course, impossible. If both players make all of the right moves in a game of chess—a game in which there may be thousands of possible right moves—then the game must, by definition, end in a draw. But both players will not make *all* of the right moves; at least one will falter. That's the skill level at work. The game may still end in a draw, or even go to the less talented player. That's the influence of random chance.

Since we can't eliminate randomness from our equations, we must try to quantify it. Let us use an example from baseball, that most quantifiable of sports. If a ball is hit to perennial Gold Glove–winning second baseman Ryne Sandberg, the "chances are" that he will field it cleanly. Actually, we can do a lot better than that: as of the end of the 1991 season, Sandberg's career fielding average stood at .988; out of many thousands of balls hit to him, he has successfully handled 99 percent of them without error. But who is to say that in this particular case he will field the ball flawlessly? This may be the one he boots. It's always possible that a random pebble on the base path will cause a bad bounce or that the ball will hit a seam in the Astroturf or a bare spot in the grass; any one of a number of seemingly insignificant, unpredictable circumstances may be in play on this particular ball and cause Sandberg to err, making him all the more human. We are, however, able to quantify his chances of success on *all* balls hit to him—based on his skill as measured by his fielding average—if not on this particular ball.

Unfortunately, an athletic contest between two teams has infinitely more immeasurable quantities to consider. For if baseballs take funny bounces, footballs take even funnier ones. The secret lies in finding some way of factoring both random chance and skill into our handicapping analysis.

The best way of doing this is a very sophisticated technique called "computer modeling," or simulation. The greatest benefit the computer brings to mankind is its ability to tirelessly repeat procedures at high speed, repetitive tasks that humans have neither the time nor the patience to perform.

The first time I ever heard of this technique being used in sports handicapping was through a neighbor. This guy has an uncle—we'll call him Jack—who is a retired computer programmer living in Florida. It seems that a friend enticed Uncle Jack to a jai alai fronton for an evening of recreational gambling. Like everyone who tries this game for the first time, Jack won a little or lost a little. It doesn't matter which, but he was struck by one seductive point: although the results were seemingly random, jai alai was at bottom a game of skill; and skill can be quantified. So Jack fired up his Apple and wrote a sophisticated computer program. Designed to reduce the randomness of the results, his software simulated—"modeled"—the playing of jai alai games many times over, as many as 40,000 per night. This is called an "iterative" process because with each repetition— or iteration—the numbers are refined and the result of the next iteration becomes more predictable.

So successful was Uncle Jack with his initial bets, that he took an apartment halfway between Dania Jai Alai and the Miami fronton. From there, daily trips to both places to make his bets and collect his winnings were easy. And so were the winnings. Jack netted between $2,500 and $3,000 a week until there was a players strike and the owners brought in amateur scabs. This drastically reduced the skill level and introduced a new, less predictable element of randomness into the game. And the modeling program ceased to be profitable. Last we heard, Uncle Jack had shifted his activities to the racetrack, where he is prospering as the handicapper for a legal betting syndicate.

George Ignatin also uses a computer modeling method in formulating his Power Ratings for football. Known as "the Professor," George can be heard on the radio and his own 900 telephone number with his picks of the day. In real life, George is an associate professor of economics at the University of Alabama at Birmingham, where, among other things, he teaches a course on "The Economics of Gambling," which relies heavily on football forecasting models. He and his sidekick, Alan Barra, who is a contributing editor to the *Village Voice*, have developed a number of innovative and insightful handicapping techniques.

The first step in their approach is the "Power Rating," the yardstick by which a handicapper can compare the relative strengths and weaknesses of two opponents. Power Ratings can be found in a number of places: Mort Olshan's *Gold Sheet*, *USA Today*, *The Green Sheet*, and even that "paper of record," *The New York Times*.

Olshan's power ratings have become an industry-wide tool, depended on by the likes of Amarillo Slim Preston and Lem Banker in their own handicapping regimens. So widespread has their use become that Olshan, fearful of giving the oddsmakers too much of an edge over his subscribers, the grassroots gamblers, once decided to suspend publication of them. But the subscribers—the very ones he was trying to protect—complained so loudly at the loss of their numbers that he quickly had to restore them.

Unlike the *Gold Sheet* ratings, which are formulated by Olshan and a staff of experts who review them weekly throughout the season, George Ignatin uses a sophisticated computer modeling program to make his numbers. The program makes a systematic analysis of all prior, relevant games. This model tries to adjust for the fact that each game is in some way unique and that teams change over time due to injuries, experience, coaching, and personnel developments, and a host of things they can't measure but whose *effects* they try to. The model also seeks to measure the effects of meeting different quality opponents in different places. It is designed not to overcompensate for a particularly good—or bad—game.

MAD MAX—or just plain MAX, as Ignatin affectionately calls his computer program—is fed the scores of all games involving the teams in the model. MAX then plays the "season" (all games already played) 50 to 100 times. Each repetition predicts the score of each game and adjusts the Power Rating and Home Field Advantage based on the actual score. The Power Rating is the raw estimate of a team's strength. The Home Field Advantage or HEDGE (shorthand for *H*ome EDGE) is a measure of the *difference* between a team's Power Rating at home and its Power Rating on the road. (Actually, Ignatin calls it HFADV, for Home Field AdVantage. As charter members of SQUASH, the Society to Quell Unpronounceable Acronyms Sharply and Harshly, we'll stick with HEDGE.) Simply put, HEDGE is the part of the equation that measures a team's performance at home against its effectiveness on the road. (Table 2.3 provides NFL Home-Field Advantage Statistics.)

TABLE 2.3: NFL HOME-FIELD ADVANTAGE
Home 'Dogs vs. Spread

Team	1989		1990	
	Straight Up	*vs. Spread*	*Straight Up*	*vs. Spread*
Atlanta	1–5	2–4	1–1	1–1
			*1–1	*1–1
Buffalo	1–0	1–0	0–0	0–0
Chicago	1–0	1–0	0–0	0–0
Cincinnati	0–0	0–0	1–1	2–0
Cleveland	1–0	1–0	0–4	0–4
			*1–0	*1–0
Dallas	0–8	2–6	4–3	5–2
Denver	0–0	0–0	0–2	0–2
Detroit	3–3	3–3	1–2	1–2
Green Bay	3–3	3–3	1–2	1–2
Houston	0–0	0–0	1–1	2–0

TABLE 2.3 (cont.)

Team	1989 Straight Up	vs. Spread	1990 Straight Up	vs. Spread
Indianapolis	2–1	2–1	3–3	3–3
	*1–0	*1–0		
Kansas City	1–1	2–0	1–0	1–0
	*0–1	*0–1		
L.A. Raiders	2–0	2–0	1–0	1–0
L.A. Rams	1–1	1–1	0–2	0–2
Miami	1–1	2–0	1–0	1–0
Minnesota	0–0	0–0	1–1	2–0
			*1–1	*1–1
New England	2–2	3–1	0–6	1–5
			*0–1	*0–1
New Orleans	1–3	1–2–1	0–1	1–0
New York Giants	0–0	0–0	0–0	0–0
New York Jets	0–3	0–3	1–3	1–3
Philadelphia	1–0	1–0	1–0	1–0
Phoenix	0–4	0–4	0–5	3–2
Pittsburgh	1–4	1–4	1–1	1–1
			*1–0	*1–0
San Diego	3–2	3–2	0–3	0–2–1
San Francisco	0–0	0–0	0–0	0–0
Seattle	1–1	1–1	2–0	2–0
	*1–0	*1–0		
Tampa Bay	2–5	4–3	2–2	2–2
Washington	1–0	1–0	0–1	0–1
Totals		37–35		33–33

NOTE: Pick-'em games, Equivalent of home 'dogs, i.e., on neutral field, would be 'dog.

(*Green Bay excludes games in Milwaukee; Indianapolis excludes games in Baltimore; LA Raiders excludes games in Oakland; LA Rams excludes games in LA Coliseum; Miami Dolphins series includes games at Joe Robbie Stadium only; Minnesota Vikings series includes games at Metrodome only; New York Jets excludes games at Shea Stadium; Phoenix Cardinals excludes games in St. Louis. And all teams' games from 1987 strike season are excluded.)

The Mad Max Power Rating also incorporates an estimate of "acceleration." As Ignatin is fond of pointing out, "This is what announcers, analysts, reporters and other innumerates inaccurately call 'momentum.' The definition of momentum is mass times velocity, which enabled Bo Jackson to run over Brian Bosworth at the Seahawks goal line in 1988." The definition of acceleration is "the rate of increase of velocity per unit of time."

In other words, Mad Max is not interested in the influence of the old "twelfth man on the field, Moe Mentum." Instead, he looks to measure acceleration, *changes* in velocity. Each week approaching the 1989 playoffs, the San Francisco 49ers raised their game a notch. Ignatin points out, "That's what we want to assess: where the team is and where it's going."

To see how the program operates, look at Table 2.4 which lists the teams in the NFL by their final (after playoffs) 1989 Power Ratings. No one should be surprised by the 49ers' large margin over the number two team, the Los Angeles Rams; nor should anyone be shocked by the Rams' number two ranking.

TABLE 2.4: 1990 SEASON
(Regular Season Games Only)

Rank	Team	Power Rating	Home Field Advantage
1.	Buffalo	110.1	1.5
2.	Kansas City	108.1	1.4
3.	Houston	107.7	3.4
4.	Philadelphia	107.0	3.2
5.	L.A. Raiders	106.5	0.7
6.	San Francisco	106.5	0.7
7.	N.Y. Giants	105.9	1.9
8.	Washington	104.2	3.3
9.	Seattle	103.9	1.6
10.	Miami	103.8	1.3
11.	Minnesota	102.2	2.1
12.	San Diego	101.8	1.5
13.	Pittsburgh	101.7	3.4
14.	Chicago	101.0	2.0
15.	Denver	100.3	1.2
16.	Detroit	99.4	1.3
17.	Cincinnati	98.6	2.4
18.	New Orleans	98.4	1.2
19.	Dallas	97.7	2.4
20.	Indianapolis	97.1	0.2
21.	Atlanta	96.9	3.2
22.	Phoenix	95.2	2.8
23.	New York Jets	94.5	−0.6
24.	L.A. Rams	94.3	1.2
25.	Green Bay	94.1	1.7
26.	Tampa Bay	92.6	1.8

TABLE 2.4 (cont.)

Rank	Team	Power Rating	Home Field Advantage
27.	Cleveland	85.6	0.7
28.	New England	84.5	2.4

(Includes All Regular Season and Playoff Games Except Super Bowl)

Rank	Team	Power Ratings	Home Field Advantage
1.	Buffalo	113.1	1.8
2.	N.Y. Giants	108.7	1.8
3.	San Francisco	107.4	0.8
4.	Kansas City	106.8	1.3
5.	Philadelphia	105.6	2.6
6.	Houston	105.4	3.9
7.	Washington	104.8	3.2
8.	Miami	103.8	1.3
9.	Seattle	103.9	1.6
10.	L.A. Raiders	103.7	1.5
11.	Minnesota	102.2	2.1
12.	San Diego	101.8	1.5
13.	Cincinnati	101.8	3.0
14.	Pittsburgh	101.7	3.4
15.	Denver	100.3	1.2
16.	Chicago	99.7	2.6
17.	Detroit	99.4	1.3
18.	Dallas	97.7	2.4
19.	New Orleans	97.6	1.4
20.	Indianapolis	97.1	0.2
21.	Atlanta	96.9	3.2
22.	Phoenix	95.2	2.8
23.	N.Y. Jets	94.5	−0.6
24.	L.A. Rams	94.3	1.2
25.	Green Bay	94.1	1.7
26.	Tampa Bay	92.6	1.8
27.	Cleveland	85.6	0.7
28.	New England	84.5	2.4

NOTE: Thus, if Buffalo hosted the New York Giants, the Bills would figure to win by 8 points. If the Giants hosted the Bills, the Bills figure to win by 0.8 of a point. And if the game were played on a neutral field, the Bills figure to win by 4.2 points.

After the Super Bowl, the figures now looked like this for the Bills and Giants:

Buffalo	112.1	2.0
N.Y. Giants	109.5	1.9

If the Super Bowl were replayed, Buffalo should win by 2.6 (112.1 − 109.5)

But how did the Cincinnati Bengals, an 8–8 team, finish third? By coming on like gangbusters in December. Check out the Houston Oilers, who finished 22d after going into a free-fall—particularly versus the Bengals. The number-four team, the New Orleans Saints, had to play the number-one and number-two teams twice each. Their 1–3 record in those games is better than almost any other team would have done.

How do you use these figures? Simple. Let's say the Kansas City Chiefs are playing the Redskins in Washington. Add up the home team's Power Rating and HEDGE: 104.2 *plus* 3.3 equals 107.5. Subtract from this the total of Kansas City's Power Rating *minus* their HEDGE: 108.1 *minus* 1.4 equals 106.7. The result makes Washington a one-point favorite, virtually pick 'em. If you can get three points with either team, you're looking at—if not exactly an overlay—certainly a live betting opportunity.

Let's take a more extreme example. The Giants are playing host to Tampa Bay. The Giants are favored by more than two touchdowns. (The Power Rating is 17.0.) This means they may be a good bet at − 14, while the Bucs may be worth a wager at +20.

We must emphasize the word *may*. All these Power Ratings and HEDGEs amount to are a method of *evaluating* the two opponents in a contest. The ratings are *not* absolutes, they are relative values used to evaluate the two teams today. As such, they make up the opening sally in the handicapping process, just the qualifying round.

The handicapping process is a little like a wine tasting: you sample a little of everything before you decide which bottle you'd like to open. If no bet is indicated at this stage of the game, you can stop right here; often this much analysis is enough to decide *against* a wager. If you've a mind to bet one of the contestants—let's say you bleed maize and blue as a fanatic graduate of the University of Michigan—and the numbers are running against the Wolverines today, you'll be well advised to drop the idea now; there will be plenty of opportunities to bet with your heart some other day, when the numbers favor your wager.

But if the numbers look favorable, it is time to consider other aspects of handicapping, intangibles not reducible to raw figures. As the saying goes, "If you live by the numbers, you die by the numbers."

If you want to emulate the Mad Max method, begin the season using the figures in Table 2.4. Then make adjustments based on two general principles:

1. Move each team's Power Rating one-third of the way toward the conference average or median.

In statistics this technique is called "regressing to the mean." It's kind of like a teacher grading on the curve. It's an effective technique because there is an inherent tendency for all teams in strong conferences to play well against outside opposition. The opposite, of course, is true of weaker conferences. This helps explain, in part, why teams like the Detroit Lions of the NFL's NFC Central Division and the University of Oregon of the PAC-10, relatively ordinary teams in tough conferences, move up a notch when facing nonconference opponents.

2. Adjust each team's Power Rating based on personnel changes (graduation losses, retirements, trades, returning starters, and so forth).

Before the 1988 season, all of the experts predicted that West Virginia would be a much improved team, mainly because the offensive line had improved over the 1987 season and was returning intact in '88. Of course, it didn't hurt that their fine quarterback, Major Harris, was also returning. Before the 1989 season, the entire line graduated, and everybody lowered their estimates for the Mountaineers' 1990 Power Rating.

Be especially careful in assessing personnel changes at the beginning of the pro season. "Plan B" free agency and other developments have made NFL rosters extremely unstable. In the past, most preseason evaluation focused on the college draft and the effects of age. Now more than a third of the roster is unprotected at the end of the season and the bidding process for journeyman players has become highly competitive. The effect has been that personnel continuity is greatly diluted from one year to the next. This has made the handicapper's task far more complex—and risky.

Another word of caution before you go racing off to the Sports Book window like an old warhorse at the sound of the bugle: a little restraint is in order. Let the form establish itself. During the early season take the opportunity to revise your numbers to reflect current form. Adjust the ratings from week to week based on how well each team does relative to its opponents. An example: if your numbers have indicated that Southern Cal should win by 21 at home and they only win by 10, you must consider reducing USC's Power Rating and HEDGE, while at the same time increasing the opponent's Power Rating and reducing its HEDGE.

Once your Power Ratings have identified some "live" bets, the next step is to qualify them. A number of factors will enter into this part of your analysis, although their relative importance will vary from game to game. The good news is that the arithmetic is already done, but this is where the real thinking begins, because here is where you will have to exercise some judgment.

First of all, you must evaluate both teams' passing games. Alan Barra argues persuasively that passing is the essential element in modern football. "In 1978, the NFL initiated rule changes in blocking and coverage which liberalized the passing game," he points out. "Yards per pass, probably pro football's most important single stat, shot way up, interceptions went down, scores swelled, and fans started turning their TV sets back on—which was the point of changing the rules in the first place."

To put this in the proper perspective, consider the history of the Super Bowl. Table 2.5 shows the final scores for the first twelve games:

TABLE 2.5: SUPER BOWL, 1967–1978

Year	Teams	Score	Total Points
1967	Green Bay-K.C.	35–10	45
1968	Green Bay-Oak.	33–14	47
1969	NY Jets-Balt.	16–7	23
1970	K.C.-Minn.	23–7	30
1971	Balt.-Dallas	16–13	29
1972	Dallas-Miami	24–3	27
1973	Miami-Wash.	14–7	21
1974	Miami-Minn.	24–7	31
1975	Pitts.-Minn.	16–6	22
1976	Pitts.-Dallas	21–17	38
1977	Oakland-Minn.	32–14	46
1978	Dallas-Denver	27–10	37

You don't have to be a statistician to see that this era was dominated by defense: the average point total was 33; not one total score cracked 50, and, of the three games that exceeded 40 points, two were played in '67 and '68 when the AFL had not yet pulled even with the NFL

Now look at what happened when teams got used to the new passing rules (see Table 2.6):

TABLE 2.6: SUPER BOWL, 1968–1991

Year	Teams	Score	Total Points
1979	Pitts.-Dallas	35–31	66
1980	Pitts.-L.A. Rams	31–19	50
1981	Oak.-Phil.	27–10	37
1982	San Fran.-Cin.	26–21	47
1983	Wash.-Miami	27–17	44
1984	L.A. Raiders-Wash.	38–9	47
1985	San Fran.-Miami	38–16	54
1986	Chi.-New England	46–10	56
1987	NY Giants-Denver	39–20	59
1988	Wash.-Denver	42–10	52

TABLE 2.6 (*cont.*)

Year	Teams	Score	Total Points
1989	San Fran.-Cin.	20–16	36
1990	San Fran.-Denver	55–10	65
1991	N.Y. Giants-Buffalo Bills	20–19	39

The 13 games averaged 50 points, 17 more than the first 12; seven games reached or topped 50 points; two exceeded 60. Not one dipped below 36, three more than the average of the first twelve games! And this is just the Super Bowl. Game-by-game and season-to-season stats also demonstrate that in the last 12 years, offense has ruled. To quote Barra: "In the modern NFL— and in major college football, too, which liberalized its passing rules in 1980—*offense is passing.*"

So marked has this trend become that, after only four weeks of the 1990 season, *Sports Illustrated* published a cover story penned by Paul Zimmerman entitled "Out of the Running." Zimmerman not only charted the decline in rushing yardage starting with the 1978 rule changes, he also showed the drop-off in 100-yard games from 1989. He cited many factors as being responsible: superior athletes on defense, the return to the 4–3 line, and holdouts and free agency, which have hampered offensive line cohesiveness, among others. He concluded that football is cyclical in nature and that the rushing game will bounce back. I think he missed the point. His own figures bear out Barra's contention that the modern game is a passing game. These other factors simply conspire to increase that development.

Of course, public opinion, which long ago lost its virginity, stubbornly clings to the outdated notion that rushing is the most important element in pro football strategy. But think about it for a moment. How often have the truly great runners— O. J. Simpson, Earl Campbell, Eric Dickerson—made it to the Super Bowl? Answer: only once. The Bears' Walter Payton finally made it to the big game just two seasons before he retired. And this was only after the Bears had finally come out of hibernation and adopted a passing attack. They also led the NFL in yards per pass that year, the only season during his years with the Bears in which Jim McMahon managed to avoid injury.

Recognizing the significance of passing is essential to understanding modern football. "To be blunt," Barra insists, "passing *is* modern football." If you want to pick winners, shed your prejudices here: no matter what your high school coach told you and no matter what you hear from TV commentators, *you do not have to establish the run to win in the NFL.* You don't even have to establish the run to win in most big-time college games. The modern pattern for winning is: pass early, opening things up late in the first and second quarters; take a lead into the locker room at halftime and in the second half rely on your pass defense to gang up on an offense that's forced to play catch-up. Run the ball as much as possible in the second half, to keep the clock running. You don't run to *gain* a lead, you run to *protect* a lead. There's no evidence over the last 32 seasons that winning teams run the ball any *better* than losing teams—they just get more *chances* because they're usually winning late in the game and trying to run down the clock.

To put it another way, the Dallas Cowboys didn't win 31 of 32 games (or whatever Frank Gifford's favorite stat on "Monday Night Football" was) because Tony Dorsett rushed for more than 100 yards; Tony Dorsett rushed for 100 yards *because* Dallas won 31 of 32. This is not to demean Dorsett. He contributed mightily to his team's victories, but his contribution was in protecting the lead once they got it, sometimes with "garbage yards" long after the fact. This is no chicken-egg situation; winning teams are not winning because they accumulate the most rushing yards, they're accumulating the most rushing yards because they're winning. In short, *games make stats, stats don't make games.*

In the NFL, almost everybody rushes for four yards a try— good teams, bad teams, mediocre teams. The fact is, *all* foot soldiers average around four yards a carry—Simpson, 4.7; Payton, 4.4; Dorsett, 4.3; Harris, 4.1; Riggins, 3.9. The real difference is in how well they pass and defend against the pass. Want to get an idea of how to tell if a team is going to pick up steam in the second half of the season? Let Barra answer that: "Look at *how well* they pass. Not how often or how many yards they accumulate, but how well. And how well they pass is indicated by football's most important and most overlooked stat: *Yards Per Pass,* both *most* yards gained per pass on offense and *least* yards allowed per pass on defense."

Need more convincing? Let's go back to the Super Bowl and look at the teams that have played for the big one over the last twelve years. (See Table 2.7.)

TABLE 2.7

Year	Teams	Yards Per Pass Rank (Rank in conference)
1979	Pittsburgh	1st
	Dallas	2nd
1980	Pittsburgh	1st
	LA Rams	8th
1981	Oakland	7th
	Philadelphia	1st
1982	San Francisco	3rd
	Cincinnati	2nd
1983	Washington	2nd
	Miami	13th
1984	LA Raiders	5th
	Washington	2nd
1985	San Francisco	1st
	Miami	1st
1986	Chicago	1st
	New England	4th
1987	NY Giants	5th
	Denver	9th
1988	Washington	2nd
	Denver	5th
1989	San Francisco	2nd
	Cincinnati	1st
1990	San Francisco	1st
	Denver	15th
1991	New York Giants	1st
	Buffalo	2nd

That's a very easy chart to read. What it says, quite simply, is this:

1. Of the more than 26 teams to play in the Super Bowl, nine—one-third—finished first in their conference in yards per pass.
2. Seven of the remaining 17 teams finished second in yards per pass.
3. 22 of the 26 teams finished in the top half of the league in yards per pass.

What the chart doesn't tell you is that the four Super Bowl teams that *did not* pass well had *pass defenses* that ranked near the top. Case in point: Denver was third in fewest yards-per-pass allowed on defense in 1983, a fact that explains their Super Bowl berth a lot better than John Elway. And the team with the worst passing offense on the list, the 1983 Dolphins—13th of the 14 AFC teams in yards gained per pass—was more than balanced by a defense that ranked first in fewest yards allowed per pass. "Whether you do it on offense or defense and, since 1978, more winning teams have been doing it on offense," says Barra, "you win by getting more yards per pass than your opponents."

Check out the Monday morning stats: anywhere from two-thirds to three-quarters of the winning teams will average more yards-per-pass than their opponents. There's no doubt about it: the running attack has no more effect on the outcome of a game than a deck chair blowing off the deck of the QE2 has on the course of the ship.

Now, I'm not saying that there's no more to winning football than that. If an underdog blocks two punts or pulls off a couple of long kickoff returns or recovers four fumbles, these are the slingshots David used to upset Goliath. But most of the time it's wise—to paraphrase Ring Lardner—to take Goliath and give the points.

Nor should coaches neglect their special teams. We're just saying that in the modern NFL, almost everybody does these things well and at about the same level of proficiency. You can't really tell anything about a team's *strength* if it misses three field goals or drops a couple of punts, and you can't count on it happening every week.

Take fumbles, for instance. Despite what you've always been told, the truth is that, year in and year out, bad teams don't fumble any more than good ones. Fumbles are just a matter of luck, and so is recovering them. Case in point: the 1989 San Francisco 49ers. Simple common sense dictates that anything they did poorly should not be counted as particularly important. Well, the Niners recovered a total of 29 fumbles, theirs and their opponents'. No fewer than 12 NFL teams did better than that, including such powerhouses as the Colts (36), and the Raiders (31).

The statmasters lump fumbles and interceptions together as "turnovers," but the 49ers' fumbles tell you nothing about their strengths. On the other hand, they led the league both ways in interceptions: giving up the fewest on offense (11), while making the most on defense (21). Stats like that tell you they were winners even if you never saw their won-lost record.

But don't expect these so-called breaks to even out in college football. Teams that run option offenses like the "wishbone" fumble far more often than those that don't. Also, with the greater disparity between the best teams and the worst, less proficient teams can be expected to fumble more often than their betters. So "net fumbles recovered" is a more reliable gauge of prowess in the college ranks than it is in the pros.

As you shall see, the passing angle is especially important in post-season handicapping, but keep it in mind for now as the principal factor to consider in regular-season play as well.

Probably the next most important weekly handicapping consideration—and probably the most misunderstood—is that of injuries. Although the NFL has long had a policy of reporting injuries early in the week, the system is not very well policed and quite vulnerable to violation. Harvey Araton of the New York *Daily News* calls the injury report nothing more than a "press release" for the NFL, an opinion shared by George Ignatin, who says, "There are lots of instances when they report guys as questionable and they're in the hospital; others play the whole game." And this is not just with some teams or individuals. "One famous case is Bill Maas, the Kansas City center," Ignatin continues. "One year he was questionable or doubtful for every game and he started every single one."

Because of the chronic violations, obtaining good information on injuries is extremely important. And when you have it, Ignatin's advice is to bet *on* the team that has suffered a widely publicized injury to a star player in a skilled position, like quarterback, and to bet *against* teams that have suffered "cluster" injuries to several players at complementary positions.

What? Doesn't that fly right in the face of conventional wisdom? Not really, it's just a matter of zigging when everyone else is determined to zag. During our conversation with the old Kentucky oddsmaker Ed Curd, we asked him about his approach to injuries and he recalled the following story:

> You can get in a great deal of trouble by Joe Blow being out of the game. The rest of the team plays that much harder. He also might not be that much of a loss to the team, even though he's supposed to be a star.
>
> I remember a situation. SMU was playing Kentucky the following Saturday and this feller from Texas called me up and he give me two dimes on Kentucky and he said, "Now, you do what you want to do, but Doak Walker will not even dress for the game."
>
> This was in 1949. Walker had won the Heisman Trophy the previous year as college football's top star and then spent most of '49 on the sidelines injured.
>
> Well, the game was about 17 points, SMU over Kentucky. And I went out and made a good bet . . . took the 17 points.

The game went down to about 13 points; then it went to 12.

Well, Walker didn't dress, but one of them Rote boys, Kyle or the other one, filled his shoes, don't you know. He ran like a wild man and I think they beat Kentucky [by] about 35 points.

Even the old oddsmaker was tripped up by what looked like a good thing. After he got his bet in at what seemed to be an attractive price, he sat back and watched the action confirm it. The bookies kept dropping the price: down to 13, and then even 12! All they were doing was reacting to the influx of Kentucky money. But public money is not always smart money; nobody thought to find out what else the Southern Methodist coach had in the barn. Anyway, we'll lay odds that Ed Curd hasn't made that mistake again over the last 40 years.

Timing is also important: if Joe Montana was injured last Sunday, everybody knows he will not play next Sunday; Steve Young will take the snaps in practice and the whole team—offense and defense—will try to exert extra effort to win. On the other hand, if Montana is supposed to start and he wakes up on Sunday morning with the flu, the Niners will be in trouble.

The most recent example of a team stepping up its game to compensate for the loss of a key player took place near the end of the 1990 NFL season. When quarterback Phil Simms went down with a sprained ankle, the team confounded the experts by sweeping through the playoffs and winning the Super Bowl behind backup quarterback Jeff Hostetler.

George Ignatin's point about clusters of injuries is also essential to identify. It's much more difficult to replace a whole unit than a single individual. If, say, the starting strong safety and a cornerback are injured and replaced by raw rookies, it may just be a Sunday afternoon stroll for the quarterback—he may never even have to drop back, let alone scramble; just dump the ball over the line to the tight end and sit back and enjoy the view.

Ignatin recalls the situation a few years ago when the Washington Redskins' offensive line was decimated by injuries; almost the entire unit was out. For three weeks the linemakers failed to adjust the spread. Then, on "Monday Night Football," with the whole world watching, Lawrence Taylor sacked quarterback Joe Theismann, snapping his leg like kindling wood. The following week the oddsmakers adjusted the line for Theismann's injury while ignoring the fact that at the same time several of the disabled linemen had recovered enough to play. To most of the public, it was amazing how well the 'Skins played with an unknown quarterback, Jay Schroeder. To those who were aware that "the Hogs," one of the best offensive lines of all time, were healthy again, it came as no surprise.

Back in 1965, one of the great Baltimore Colt teams of the era thought their season had gone south when first quarterback Johnny Unitas and then his backup, Earl Morrall, succumbed to injuries. Undaunted, the Colts turned to running back Tom Matte, who had been a quarterback in high school and, briefly, on a Woody Hayes run-oriented Ohio State squad. Matte wrote the plays on his wristband, but Don Shula would send in a fresh guard with a play on every down anyway, presumably not just to tell Matte what to *call*, but also what to *do*. Matte and the Colts survived to the division championship game, which they barely lost to the Green Bay Packers.

In college games, single injuries to key players can be far more critical. When Washington State quarterback Brad Gossen was hurt, the Cougars were forced to turn to a freshman and it was the end of their season. Sometimes, however, the importance of such injuries is not so immediately apparent. When Miami's starting quarterback, Craig Erickson, was hurt in 1989, freshman Gino Torretta stepped in to take his place. Because of the Hurricanes' wealth of talent at other positions, the effect wasn't noticeable until they played Florida State. Then Toretta's lack of experience cost them six turnovers and the ball game. Adversity also can be a great motivator. When Alabama quarterback Jeff Dunn was hurt, the Tide turned to Gary Hollingsworth, who didn't know the complicated offense. Forced to simplify their play book, the coaching staff stressed passing, and that's what put them into the Sugar Bowl.

One of the most abused concepts in sports handicapping is that of "trends." Although they have their place, trends are all too often misunderstood and misapplied. The great Apostle of the Trend was the late Pete Axthelm, who used to flog his black arts on "The NFL Today" and ESPN's "SportsCenter." Pete was known to say something like, "Everybody knows the Eagles are 6–1 against the spread when playing on the road versus an NFC central division team the week after losing to an AFC team." The obvious problems with this conclusion are:

1. With only seven observations, there just aren't enough games to draw any valid conclusions.
2. Even if there had been a large enough number, he's equating Lions and Bears. If the games occurred over 10 or 20 years, as is likely, the Eagles could have played the Bucs, Lions and Packers in recent years, the Bears in the '70s and the Vikings in the '60s.
3. Moreover, the majority of the seven games might have involved the Ron Jaworski Eagles, not the current Randall Cunningham–Jim McMahon model.

Obviously, this kind of thinking can get you in trouble. There have, however, been some very strong, relatively recent trends that have worked and also illustrate an important point: by the time a trend is apparent to the betting public, the linemakers are aware of it, too.

At once the best-known and longest-lived trend in the NFL involves Monday night games (see Table 2.8). The rule: bet on home team underdogs. Even though Las Vegas is obviously aware of this trend, it continued to work through 1989—but, as with many trends, it was less than successful the next year. When the Buffalo Bills, playing without Jim Kelly, upset the

Rams as home 'dogs, the linemakers overreacted. The following week they made Denver a four-point favorite over the visiting Redskins in what normally would have been a pick 'em game. But what is true for home team 'dogs is not necessarily true for home favorites, and the 'Skins won the game straight-up.

For several years prior to the 1989 season, road favorites switching from turf to grass or vice versa rolled up an uncanny 27–1 record against the spread. With a trend like that, anyone can make money. Or so the bookies thought. Week after week, the spread on road favorites switching surfaces kept getting bigger and bigger. Then, during the 1989 season, the angle seemed to lose its potency, although it still bears watching.

Is the Grass Really Greener?

Is change of turf a relevant variable in handicapping the NFL? Perhaps not. Interestingly, teams that normally play on natural grass perform slightly better in domed stadiums than do teams that play their home games on artificial turf.

During the eighties, natural grass teams beat the spread 53.7 percent of the time indoors. Dome visitors who normally play on a rug at home were successful 53.5 percent. The difference is insignificant, but it points up the fact that moving indoors is not an automatic reason to eliminate a team. In fact, if the team in question is the Philadelphia Eagles, they're practically an automatic bet. Going into the 1991 season, the Eagles are 9–1 under a dome.

During the 1986 season, the Detroit Lions compiled an extraordinary record against the spread. They covered the point spread in seven out of eight games at home and their road record was almost a mirror image; they were just as bad away as they were good at home. Since then, the Lions have done just the opposite, playing much better on the road than at home. What happened? No one knows for sure, but it might be that the Lions, aware of the trend, assumed that they didn't need to worry about home games but worked extra hard for away games. Or their opponents might have worked overtime preparing for games in Pontiac. Or both might have happened. Or the whole thing might have been a fluke.

Often what happened in the past is simply irrelevant. A classic example is the Chicago Bears–Washington Redskins championship game of 1940. In one of the last games of the season the two teams had met and Washington had won, 7–3. Naturally they were favored in the rematch for the title. And what happened? The scoreboard attendant became a candidate for disability pay as he logged in a 73–0 win for the "Monsters of the Midway," thereby proving the mutability of temporal affairs.

Reversals of form of this magnitude are not particularly common, but there are enough similar incidents to cause us to haul out the old red danger flag. Here are just a few cases from the 1990 season. Before their first meeting, the New England Patriots had won seven of the last 11 from the Cincinnati Bengals. Big deal! The Bengals won their next game, 41–7. Southern Cal had not lost a conference game since 1987 going into its game with the University of Washington; Washington won 31–0. And Clemson had beaten the University of Virginia 29 straight times. Result: UVA 20, Clemson 7. At some point, the contrarian in all of us should kick in and say, bet the other way!

Certainly there are some trends that bear watching, such as the fact that, through 1989, the Denver Broncos won 23 of their last 28 home games against AFC West opponents, or that the Raiders have the best "Monday Night Football" record at 29–6–1. But some of these can get downright silly. Did you know, for instance, that under Joe Paterno, Penn State is 42–3 against opponents with ornithological names through 1990? That's right. Teams with names like Owls and Eagles, Hawkeyes and Jayhawks, all turn to flightless dodos at the feet of the Nittany

Lions. And if you think that's enough information to make a wager, you don't need this book.

Clearly, to rely on these trends without further study is worse than a crime. What happened in the past, to paraphrase George Santayana, is mere prologue; but, as one writer so aptly points out, a trend handicapper is like a weather forecaster using the Farmer's Almanac instead of meteorological instruments. Just because it happened before, when the teams or the players were different, doesn't mean it will happen again. (See Table 2.8 for home opener trends, an example of historical data which is worthless as a betting tool.)

And that, in a nutshell, is what is wrong with most trends. The concept, like many gambling terms, comes from the world of finance and means a kind of regular irregularity. And, as many a broken-down investor who has turned a substantial stake into a somewhat smaller one can tell you, by themselves all they bring is grief. By the time the public has identified a trend, it has been thoroughly discounted, usually to the point of worthlessness.

Finally, do not mistake a longstanding record of excellence for a temporary trend. There are a few situations, particularly in college football, that have withstood the test of time to graduate from the realm of trends to that of tradition. Some schools are like blue-chip stocks. Since 1950 Oklahoma has been Number One in the Associated Press preseason poll eight times, Notre Dame and Ohio State five times each, and Nebraska four times, and more often than not, they have been there at the end of the season as well. These institutions, along with others like the University of Michigan, Penn State (Linebacker U.), and the University of Southern California (Tailback U.), have solid traditions of excellence in coaching and recruiting that have kept them at or near the top of the charts year after year.

Probably because of these traditional strengths, long-term tendencies seem to last much longer than the short-lived trends we have been considering. Sometimes they last as long as 10 or 15 years or more. Consider these trends through 1990:

Table 2.8: NFL Home Openers

Team	Straight-Up W-L	W-L Record vs. the Spread
Atlanta Falcons	6–11	7–9–1
Buffalo Bills	8–9	10–5–2
Chicago Bears	12–5	11–5–1
Cincinnati Bengals	9–8	6–10–1
Cleveland Browns	8–9	7–10
Dallas Cowboys*	14–3	13–4
Denver Broncos	13–4	10–6–1
Detroit Lions*	9–8	9–8
Green Bay Packers†	7–10	7–10
Houston Oilers	12–5	10–7
Indianapolis Colts	3–14	4–12–1
Kansas City Chiefs	9–8	11–6
Los Angeles Raiders	15–2	14–3
Los Angeles Rams	10–7	6–9–2
Miami Dolphins*	15–2	8–8–1
Minnesota Vikings	11–5–1	8–9
New England Patriots	8–9	7–10
New Orleans Saints	4–13	5–12
New York Giants	7–10	9–7–1
New York Jets	7–10	8–9
Philadelphia Eagles	8–9	6–11
Phoenix Cardinals	8–9	7–10
Pittsburgh Steelers	12–5	10–7
San Diego Chargers	11–6	10–7
San Francisco 49ers	7–10	5–10–2
Seattle Seahawks	6–8	8–6
Tampa Bay Buccaneers	5–9	5–9
Washington Redskins	12–5	9–8

*Streak game of 1987 not counted as home opener.
†Home openers at Milwaukee included.

- Alabama is the best road dog. Over the past 16 years The Crimson Tide is 12–2 in these situations.
- North Carolina State just can't seem to get started; they're 1–11 in home openers against the spread over the last 12 years.
- There is no home-field advantage or disadvantage in the Ivy League. The worst offender is Princeton, which is 9–18 as a home 'dog over the last 17 years.

- Some teams really prefer the comforts of home. Perennial powerhouse Auburn schedules most of its big games at home and is 6–13 versus the spread on the road.
- Iowa State has beaten Oklahoma only once since 1961— in 1990.
- Tennessee has only 3 losses in its last 25 games—all versus Alabama.
- Auburn's record within 50 miles of home is much different than away, with a 20-game unbeaten streak at home.
- The University of Miami has won 34 straight at the Orange Bowl.
- Florida State's average margin of victory over Tulane over the past 7 years is 35 points.

There are a few good angles, however, that work year in and year out. And it is this very fact of continuing success that removes them from the black-magic world of trends. Foremost of these is the "sandwich." When a very good team—let's call them the Lions—beats another very good team—say, the Tigers—in week one and is scheduled to play an average team—say, the Bears—in week two, followed by another very good team in week three, the Lions are "caught in a sandwich." Obviously they will not be "up" for the Bears, who will be getting points because of the Lions' victory over the Tigers. You won't find many of these betting situations, but when you do, subtract at least 7 points from your estimate of how much the Lions will beat the Bears by.

Note also that the Tigers will be seething after their loss to the Lions and will be out to undo their humiliation: add at least three points to your estimate of how well they will do in their next game.

Bad teams sometimes offer good value, particularly when a traditional rivalry is involved (see Table 2.9). When two bad teams, like Kansas and Kansas State, play, bet against the winner the following week. The winner will still be celebrating the previous week's victory when they take the field against their next opponent.

TABLE 2.9: TRADITIONAL COLLEGE RIVALRIES, THROUGH 1991

Notre Dame–Southern Cal.	Notre Dame 36–23–4
Southern Cal.–UCLA	Southern Cal. 35–20–7
Alabama-Auburn	Alabama 31–23–1
Texas-Oklahoma	Texas 50–32–4
Army-Navy	Series Tied: 42–42–7
LSU-Mississippi	LSU 44–31–4
Georgia-Florida	Georgia 44–23–2
Oklahoma-Nebraska	Oklahoma 39–29–3
Michigan–Ohio State	Michigan 49–34–5
TCU-SMU	SMU 35–29–7

Surprisingly, the pros are subject to these same kinds of emotional ups and downs. The problem is identifying them. Simple rules, like "Bet against a good team facing two division foes surrounding a non-conference opponent," are not specific enough; if the 49ers play New Orleans, Cincinnati, and Atlanta, in that order, do you really think they'll look past the Bengals and be up for the Falcons? And if they lose to the Bengals, would you want to write the Falcons' workers compensation policy?

Finally, what do we do when it's all over but the shouting? Although the NFL playoffs regularly produce good games—and good *betting* games—increasingly the Super Bowl has become a game of blowouts. With two exceptions, every game since 1979 has been a rout (1989, the 49ers versus the Bengals, and 1991, the New York Giants versus the Buffalo Bills). All have been over by the fourth quarter if not by halftime. During the eighties, in four of the last six seasons a "super" team emerged. The 1985 Bears, the 1986 Giants and the Niners of 1984 and 1989 won the Super Bowl by a staggering combined total of 122 points. The average margin of victory was 30.5 points, and each team beat the spread easily. This has made for some pretty boring viewing for all but the astute handicapper who has found a soft spot in the biggest event of the year. The 1991 Super Bowl, however, was anything but a blowout and

1991 Super Bowl, however, was anything but a blowout and may signal a return to close—and exciting—games again. But don't bet on it!

Table 2.10: NFC AND AFC CHAMPIONSHIP GAMES (Since NFL-AFL Merger in 1970)

Year	AFC Teams and Final Scores	Favorite	Home Team
1970	Baltimore Colts 27–Oakland Raiders 17	Oak. −1	Baltimore
1971	Miami Dolphins 21–Baltimore Colts 0	Miami −1½	Miami
1972	Miami Dolphins 21–Pittsburgh Steelers 17	Miami −2½	Pittsburgh
1973	Miami Dolphins 27–Oakland Raiders 10	Miami −6½	Miami
1974	Pittsburgh Steelers 24–Oakland Raiders 13	Oak. −5½	Oakland
1975	Pittsburgh Steelers 16–Oakland Raiders 10	Pitt. −6	Pittsburgh
1976	Oakland Raiders 24–Pittsburgh Steelers 7	Pitt. −4½	Oakland
1977	Denver Broncos 20–Oakland Raiders 17	Oak. −3½	Denver
1978	Pittsburgh Steelers 34–Houston Oilers 5	Pitt. −7	Pittsburgh
1979	Pittsburgh Steelers 27–Houston Oilers 13	Pitt. −9½	Pittsburgh
1980	Oakland Raiders 34–San Diego Chargers 27	S.D. −4	San Diego
1981	Cincinnati Bengals 27–San Diego Chargers 7	Cin. −4½	Cincinnati
1982	Miami Dolphins 14–New York Jets 0	Miami −9½	Miami
1983	Los Angeles Raiders 30–Seattle Seahawks 14	L.A. −7½	Los Angeles
1984	Miami Dolphins 45–Pittsburgh Steelers 28	Miami −9½	Miami
1985	New England Patriots 31–Miami Dolphins 14	Miami −4½	Miami
1986	Denver Broncos 23–Cleveland Browns 20 (OT)	Cleve. −3	Cleveland
1987	Denver Broncos 38–Cleveland Browns 33	Denver −2½	Denver
1988	Cincinnati Bengals 21–Buffalo Bills 10	Cin. −4	Cincinnati
1989	Denver Broncos 37–Cleveland Browns 21	Denver −3½	Cleveland
1990	Buffalo Bills 51–Los Angeles Raiders 3	Buff. −6½	Buffalo

Summation

Home teams:

15–6, straight-up
15–5–1, vs. the spread
Home Favorites vs. Spread: 11–4–1
Home Underdogs vs. Spread: 3–2

	NFC		
1970	Dallas Cowboys 17–San Francisco 49ers 10	S.F. −4½	San Francisco
1971	Dallas Cowboys 14–San Francisco 49ers 3	Dallas −7½	Dallas
1972	Washington Redskins 26–Dallas Cowboys 3	Wash. −3	Washington
1973	Minnesota Vikings 27–Dallas Cowboys 10	Dallas −1	Dallas
1974	Minnesota Vikings 14–Los Angeles Rams 10	Minn. −4	Minnesota
1975	Dallas Cowboys 37–Los Angeles Rams 7	L.A. −6	Los Angeles
1976	Minnesota Vikings 24–Los Angeles Rams 13	Minn. −4½	Minnesota
1977	Dallas Cowboys 23–Minnesota Vikings 6	Dallas −11½	Dallas
1978	Dallas Cowboys 28–Los Angeles Rams 0	Dallas −3½	Los Angeles
1979	Los Angeles Rams 9–Tampa Bay Buccaneers 0	L.A. −3½	Tampa Bay
1980	Philadelphia Eagles 20–Dallas Cowboys 7	Dallas −1	Philadelphia

TABLE 2.10 (*cont.*)

Year	NFC Teams and Final Scores	Favorite	Home Team
1981	San Francisco 49ers 28–Dallas Cowboys 27	Dallas −3	San Francisco
1982	Washington Redskins 31–Dallas Cowboys 17	Dallas −2	Washington
1983	Washington Redskins 24–San Francisco 49ers 21	Wash. −10½	Washington
1984	San Francisco 49ers 23–Chicago Bears 0	S.F. −9	San Francisco
1985	Chicago Bears 24–Los Angeles Rams 0	Chi. −10	Chicago
1986	New York Giants 17–Washington Redskins 0	N.Y. −7	New York
1987	Washington Redskins 17–Minnesota Vikings 10	Wash. −2½	Washington
1988	San Francisco 49ers 28–Chicago Bears 3	S.F. −1	Chicago
1989	San Francisco 49ers 30–Los Angeles Rams 3	S.F. −7	San Francisco
1990	New York Giants 15–San Francisco 49ers 13	S.F. −9	San Francisco

Summation

Home Teams:

14–7, straight-up

13–7–1, vs. the spread

Home Favorites vs. Spread 9–5–1

Home Underdogs vs. Spread 3–3

The beauty of it is that it has been increasingly possible to spot the dominant team long before the big game. In a study of all Super Bowls played since the rules changed in 1978, Ignatin and Barra determined that:

1. By the final quarter of the season, all teams headed for the Super Bowl were at or near the top of their conference in Passing Yardage Differential (the difference between average yardage gained per pass and average yards per pass allowed).
2. Every team that played in the Super Bowl ranked first or second in Passing Yardage Differential *in the league.*

By week 12 of the 1989 season, San Francisco's passing yardage differential was 3.8. Amazing, when you consider that the number-two-ranked Rams had a 1.8! No AFC team exceeded 1.3, and Denver, the eventual AFC winner, was averaging only .7, a sure sign that the Broncos were winning on defense and *not* on John Elway's arm.

Taking advantage of their mile-high altitude, the Broncos

backed into the Super Bowl by rolling over weak opponents in the playoffs; the 49ers roared in by humiliating both Minnesota and Los Angeles, two of the best teams in the league whether measured by power ratings or by passing yardage differential; they were at least equal to and probably superior to Denver. (See Table 2.10.) The Niners ended the season with a phenomenal offensive average of 9.49 yards per throw, compared to Denver's 7.08—a breathtaking difference of nearly two and a half yards. Never in Super Bowl history had two teams shown so sharp a difference in passing performance.

Barra and Ignatin announced in the November 30 issue of the *Village Voice* that "with five weeks to go, the season is over. The 49ers will win the NFC West, march through the playoffs, and beat any AFC team unfortunate enough to meet them in New Orleans by at least 17 points." That prediction was written almost two months before the game, and Barra calls it "the easiest call we've ever made."

Although the passing stats were enough to make the Niners a solid pick, there were other reasons, good solid ones, to prefer them. Check out every "Super" team of recent years—did they ease up in the stretch or did they get stronger? Did they blow big leads or did they shut their opponents down in the second half? In 1986 the Giants and the Broncos seemed about equal after 11 weeks. In week 12 they met in the Jersey Meadowlands. The Giants won a squeaker, 19–16. They finished out the season with 4 wins and went on to trounce their two playoff opponents by a total of 63 points; Denver limped home, losing 2 out of 4 and squeaking by in two playoff games by a total of 8 points. In the Super Bowl, the Giants demolished the Broncos, the same team they had gone all out to beat six scant weeks before.

OK, you say, but each season doesn't produce a "Super" team. How do I know who the best teams are if there's no obvious Super team? Start by remembering this: *No team has ever gone to the Super Bowl that didn't average more yards per pass on offense than it gave up on defense.* Not one.

And this includes the great running teams. A case in point is the Giants, champions of Super Bowl XXV. The classic grind-it-out-on-the-ground team, they combined a conservative passing game with a superb pass defense to lead the league in Passing Yardage Differential. Interesting enough, their passing yardage stats actually improved after Jeff Hostetler took over for Phil Simms at quarterback.

And this did not just begin in 1978. Outpassing the other team *always* has been the most important element in pro football. In recent years, however, the passing game has become far more sophisticated, so margins of victory have widened. Look for teams coming down the stretch that are outpassing their opponents, not in terms of completion percentage or total yards, but measured in *yards per throw*. The team that *looks* like it's hottest at this point usually is; the team that looks like it's going all the way usually does.

Modern pro football is a game of dominance, not balance, like baseball. In baseball a powerful team may win 95 to 100 games out of 162 for a winning percentage of about .600. That's dominance in baseball. Too many factors—speed, fielding, relief pitching—keep a team from winning 140 or 150 games. There are too many checks and balances. But in the eighties, pro football regularly produced teams that finished 14–2 or 15–1. That's expected in football, where you dominate with passing and pass defense. And no amount of running or "ball control" or a "sound kicking game" is going to reduce the balance.

College coaches tend to be even more conservative than their professional counterparts, so you will hear even more about "establishing the run." Woody Hayes made "three yards and a cloud of dust" famous. But have you ever noticed what happens when a great rushing team plays a team of near equal talent that can pass? Miami wins. If running is supposed to beat passing, why did Oklahoma fail to beat Miami or even cover the spread when the national title was on the line? Before the 1990 Orange Bowl, Notre Dame ranked as high as the Hurricanes in the power ratings; Notre Dame had played a tougher schedule and had a better record. But after Miami got its first touchdown passing, the Irish were never in the game. Why? Because it was the pros against college boys—not in terms of ability, which would have shown up before the game, but in their approach to the game. Notre Dame was ready to dig in and play old-fashioned trench-war football. Miami said, in effect, no thanks, we'll have plenty of time for that when we have a big lead to protect. Once they had scored through the air, Notre Dame was in deep trouble because their option-running attack wasn't designed for catching up. Once Miami got up by *two* scores, they were happy to let their opponents run the ball. They even ran it themselves, but not until they had built a lead too big to be assaulted by a passing attack that dated from the Stone Age.

Around the turn of the century, a familiar figure in rural America appeared, that curious breed of traveling man cum con man known as the "snake oil salesman." This slick operator would wheel his one-horse circus into the rural towns of the time, drop his tailgate, and haul out his wares for any and all who would give him time. And many did, for entertainment was in short supply on the prairie.

Taking advantage of this shortage, he would tell jokes, relate

Table 2.11: COLLEGE FOOTBALL'S TEN BIGGEST UPSETS IN THE 1980s

Spread	Underdog Winner	Favorite Loser	Score	Year
36	Texas–El Paso*	Brigham Young	23–16	1985
36	Oregon State	Washington*	21–20	1985
32	Northwestern*	Minnesota	31–21	1982
26	Northwestern	Missouri*	27–23	1985
25	Minnesota	Michigan*	20–17	1986
24½	Tulane	Louisiana State*	31–28	1982
24	Syracuse*	Nebraska	17–9	1984
24	Northwestern	Michigan State*	28–24	1982
24	Georgia Tech	Alabama*	24–21	1981
24	Air Force	Brigham Young*	39–38	1982

*Home team.
SOURCE: Arne Lange

feats of derring-do, spin ghost stories, perform magic—all to attract a crowd before he got down to business. And business for him was hawking a wondrous elixir guaranteed to heal all ailments, restore youth and vigor, instill virility, and implant fertility. This was, of course, all without validity, for his product was concocted with little concern for anything but that which was handy—spring water, a little alcohol, some mud from a riverbed, perhaps some raw petroleum if he chanced to find some seeping from a rock. Some of the more high-class potions contained a few herbs for flavor, but not much. In fact, the fouler the better, for the salesman relied on the common belief that good medicine must taste bad. This and his own spellbinding talents were all he had to sell.

But that was enough to convince poorly educated, lonely farmers. Many bought the salesman's wares. By the time they figured out they'd been had, he was on the road again, selling his dreams in another town.

That was in the Old West. The New West, too, has its snake oil salesmen, only now they're called "touts." As their audience has grown more sophisticated, so have they, employing the media, the personal computer, and the telephone to sell their dreams. And though they have perhaps grown more sophisticated, the audience is at least as gullible as their pioneer ancestors.

There is, in fact, no more gullible audience anywhere than gamblers. Whether it is greed, the promise of easy money, or the forlorn despair of ever being a winner that propels them, the fact is that there is no easier mark for a modern snake oil salesman than the gambler. The tout holds out the promise of winnings far beyond any sane expectation, and yet he'll always find a taker.

The word *tout* comes down to us—as do so many gambling terms—from the racetracks of the British Isles. Originally, it was the function of the tout to obtain information about the day's entrants and sell it to the punters. At first this was a relatively honorable calling, with touts vying with one another for the reputation of having the most reliable information. But as time went by, racing grew to be big business and the touts' sources of information became available to all. Rather than give up a lucrative business altogether, the more unscrupulous began to sell phony information to whomever would pay.

And there were plenty who would. A favorite racetrack scam adopted by touts the world over revolves around what we call the "meet me" ploy. Here's how it works: Tommy the Tout picks out a likely mark, Gary Gullible, and engages him in chitchat, trying to gain his confidence. At the right moment, Tommy tells Gary that he already knows the identity of the winner of the next race. If Tommy has laid the groundwork properly, the fact that no one can know the winner before the race never will arise; instead, Gary will ask for the horse. And Tommy will give it to him. All Gary has to do is buy Tommy a $20 win ticket. If Gary agrees, Tommy will give him the horse's number and tell him, "Meet me" after the race with my winning ticket. He'll be by the hot dog stand or the escalator or the entrance to the clubhouse.

Gary heads for the mutuel window and Tommy looks around for another sucker. The object is to find one for every horse in the race so that the tout is sure to cash a winning ticket purchased by a happy client. The secret to success at this game is in remembering where you told the real winner to go. If Gary Gullible is supposed to meet Tommy at the hot dog stand, it could be dangerous for Tommy to show up if his horse lost. And he'll never tell two suckers to meet him at the same place.

A good way to spot this scam is by the numbers. The tout will tell the holder of the ticket on the one horse to meet him at the escalator; the guy with the two, at the hot dog stand, the holder of the three outside the entrance to the clubhouse, and so on. This way he can keep them all straight from race to race and from day to day without clouding his own mind with horses' names.

A modern-day turn on this old game is run by the telephone tout and revolves around modern sales techniques and an appreciation of large numbers. It often starts out with an ad in a gambling weekly; just as often it begins with a mass mailing to known gamblers. The most sophisticated scams will probably combine both of these techniques. The come-on is that our Thomas (Tommy's gone big time; he has an office now and wears a suit) will give respondents the winner of a football game absolutely free just for trying his service. And this is guaranteed—a mortal lock!

Like Thomas, Gary Gullible is a modern man. You can't fool him. But this is *free!* No strings! Why not try it? And what happens if he wins? The following week, Gary will have to pay for the service. But, knowing our Gary, he'll be eager to do it. And who can blame him? After all, he's a winner.

Thomas's profit potential is enormous because there are thousands of Garys. Let's say that Thomas mails out 10,000 sales letters promising his "mortal lock" and that he gets a respectable return, say 4 percent. That's 400 people who think they're going to be given the winner to a football game. And half of them will be right. Let's say the game is CHICAGO − 2½ over New England. Thomas will give half of the suckers the Bears and the other half the Patriots. The 200 losers will be disappointed but not hurt badly and as unlikely to sue as they are to purchase the service.

Of course, half of the lucky 200 customers are destined to lose the next week, but the other half will be more than happy to pony up again. And the mass mailings and advertising will keep up a steady flow of sheep ready for Thomas to shear.

The variations on the tout theme are legion. Some are almost legitimate. (Even with Thomas your chances are 50/50; one of his picks *is*, after all, a mortal lock.) Some are much worse. The real point is that there are a lot of unscrupulous folks out there trying to relieve you of your hard-earned cash. Don't be fooled. Experiment with your sources of information until you find the ones that you are most comfortable with; then make your own choices. No one knows the winner before they play the game.

It is said that Vegas is a town where "the over/under on weddings is twenty-four hours," and it would be wrong to conclude our football discussion without considering the over/under bet.

It has become so popular that several newspapers now post over/under lines alongside the point spread. In this wager, the bettor tries to predict whether or not the total score will exceed the oddsmakers' number. To many, it is an extension of their regular bet: if you bet the favorite, giving the points, then you will bet the over; if you take the points, you will bet the under.

Vinny Magliulo remembers one of Caesars' over/under propositions especially well. For the 1989 Indianapolis 500 he posted the number of cars that would finish at 11½. Thirty-three cars start at Indy, but mechanical failures and accidents always shrink the field drastically before they wave the checkered flag for the victor. Late in the race, Vinny was in his back office when he heard an ominous rumble coming from the Sports Book. Expecting the worst, maybe an earthquake, he hurried out to see what it was. And what to his wondering eyes should appear? Watching the huge screen was a crowd of avid punters, excitedly counting down as crashes reduced the field: ". . . nineteen . . . eighteen . . . seventeen . . ."

In football, the over/under is the wager most affected by the weather—the worse the weather, the lower the score. Or so the traditional wisdom goes. Weather doesn't normally affect the point spread much, as each team is penalized equally by the elements, but they can be expected to score proportionately less. So a Willard Scott check or a call to the local weather bureau is in order on this bet. But save your money on long-distance calls to Houston, New Orleans, Minneapolis, Detroit, and Seattle, where they play football indoors (see Table 2.12).

Another wrinkle in the over/under bet is the NFL's latest "hurry-up" offense. In answer to TV's rigid scheduling problems, they shortened the games from an average time of three hours and eleven minutes–plus in 1989 to just under three hours in 1990, with a reduction in total plays from 154 to 148. This also effectively reduced the number of points scored by each team. The oddsmakers reacted quickly, so there were no soft spots here, but by now, you should be able to make adjustments in your own betting patterns based on new rules and regulations.

TABLE 2.12: NFL WEATHER NUMBERS

Team	Stadium	Playing Surface	Weather Number
Atlanta Falcons	Atlanta–Fulton County Stadium	Natural	(404) 936-1111
Buffalo Bills	Rich Stadium	Artificial	(716) 976-1212
Chicago Bears	Soldier Field	Natural	(312) 976-1212
Cincinnati Bengals	Riverfront Stadium	Artificial	(606) 936-4850
Cleveland Browns	Municipal Stadium	Natural	(216) 931-1212
Dallas Cowboys	Irving Stadium	Artificial	(214) 993-2626
Denver Broncos	Mile High Stadium	Natural	(303) 639-1212
Detroit Lions	Pontiac Silverdome	Artificial	
Green Bay Packers	Lambeau Field;	Natural	(414) 432-1212
	Milwaukee County Stadium	Natural	(414) 936-1212
Houston Oilers	Astrodome	Artificial	
Indianapolis Colts	Hoosier Dome	Artificial	
Kansas City Chiefs	Arrowhead Stadium	Artificial	(816) 471-4840
Los Angeles Raiders	L.A. Coliseum	Natural	(213) 554-1212
Los Angeles Rams	Los Angeles Memorial	Natural	(213) 554-1212
Miami Dolphins	Joe Robbie Stadium	Natural	(305) 661-5065
Minnesota Vikings	Hubert H. Humphrey Metrodome	Artificial	
New England Patriots	Foxboro Stadium	Natural	(617) 936-1234
New Orleans Saints	Louisiana Superdome	Artificial	
New York Giants	Giants Stadium	Artificial	(201) 976-1212
New York Jets	Giants Stadium	Artificial	(201) 976-1212
Philadelphia Eagles	Veterans Stadium	Artificial	(215) 936-1212
Phoenix Cardinals	Sun Devil Stadium	Natural	(602) 957-8700
Pittsburgh Steelers	Three River Stadium	Artificial	(412) 936-1212
San Diego Chargers	Jack Murphy Stadium	Natural	(619) 289-1212

Team	Stadium	Surface	Phone
San Francisco 49ers	Candlestick Park	Natural	(415) 936-1212
Seattle Seahawks	Kingdome	Artificial	
Tampa Bay Buccaneers	Tampa Stadium	Natural	(813) 645-2506
Washington Redskins	Robert F. Kennedy Stadium	Natural	(202) 936-1212

♦ ♦ ♦

Finally, here are a few things to keep in mind when you are handicapping. They are not rules to follow slavishly, they should be used where they fit into your own gambling style:

- When in doubt, take the points.
- Don't bet against passing teams when they are big underdogs.
- Favor the home team when the game is a "no-count" game. This usually occurs when the teams' division or conference races have been decided.
- Don't bet the underdog when the spread is 2 touchdowns or more. Upsets rarely occur in these circumstances.
- Teams at the top of the college ratings cover the spread a lot more often than do teams at the bottom. Consistency is one of the hallmarks of a winner.

I hope I've been able to give you a few useful crumbs of advice. But now that you're on your own, be sure to examine every bet with an eye as critical as a horse trader's. There are fewer overlays and soft spots in football than sightings of Elvis, so do your homework and be careful.

TABLE 2.13: COLLEGE FOOTBALL:
Schools and Their Playing Surfaces

School	Conference	Stadium	Playing Surface
Air Force	WAC	Falcon	Natural
Akron	Independent	Rubber Bowl	Artificial
Alabama	Southeastern	Bryant-Denny;	Artificial
		Legion Field	Artificial
Arizona	Pacific Ten	Arizona	Natural
Arizona State	Pacific Ten	Sun Devil Stadium	Natural
Arkansas	Southwest	Razorback	Artificial
Army	Independent	Michie Stadium	Artificial
Auburn	Southeastern	Jordan-Hare Stadium	Natural
Ball State	Mid-American	Ball State	Natural
Baylor	Southwest	Floyd Casey Stadium	Artificial
Boston College	Independent	Alumni Stadium	Artificial
Bowling Green	Mid-American	Perry Field	Natural
Brigham Young	WAC	Brigham Young Stadium	Natural
California	Pacific Ten	Memorial Stadium	Artificial
Cal State–Fullerton	Big West	Santa Ana	Natural
Central Michigan	Mid-American	Kelly/Shorts	Artificial
Cincinnati	Independent	Nippert;	Artificial
		Riverfront	Artificial
Clemson	Atlantic Coast	Memorial Stadium	Natural
Colorado	Big Eight	Folsom Stadium	Artificial
Colorado State	WAC	Hughes	Natural
Duke	Atlantic Coast	Wallace Wade	Natural
East Carolina	Independent	Ficklen	Natural
Eastern Michigan	Mid-American	Rynearson	Natural

School	Conference	Stadium	Playing Surface
Florida	Southeastern	Florida Field	Natural
Florida State	Independent	Doak Campbell	Natural
Fresno State	Big West	Bulldog	Natural
Georgia	Southeastern	Sanford	Natural
Georgia Tech	Atlantic Coast	Bobby Dodd Stadium	Artificial
Hawaii	WAC	Aloha	Artificial
Houston	Southwestern	Astrodome	Artificial
Illinois	Big Ten	Memorial Stadium	Artificial
Indiana	Big Ten	Memorial Stadium	Artifical
Iowa	Big Ten	Kinnick	Natural
Iowa State	Big Eight	Trice Field	Artificial
Kansas	Big Eight	Memorial Stadium	Artificial
Kansas State	Big Eight	Kansas State University Stadium	Artificial
Kent State	Mid-American	Dix	Natural
Kentucky	Southeastern	Commonwealth	Natural
Long Beach State	Big West	Veterans	Natural
Louisville	Missouri Valley	Cardinal	Artificial
Louisiana State	Southeastern	Tiger	Natural
Louisiana Tech	Independent	Aillet	Natural
Maryland	Atlantic Coast	Byrd Stadium	Natural
Memphis State	Missouri Valley	Liberty Bowl	Natural
Miami (Florida)	Independent	Orange Bowl	Natural
Miami (Ohio)	Mid-American	Yager	Natural
Michigan	Big Ten	Michigan Stadium	Natural
Michigan State	Big Ten	Spartan	Artificial
Minnesota	Big Ten	Metrodome	Artificial
Mississippi	Southeastern	Vaught-Hemmingway Stadium	Natural

School	Conference	Stadium	Surface
Mississippi State	Southeastern	Scott Field; Memorial	Natural; Natural
Missouri	Big Eight	Faurot Field	Artificial
Navy	Independent	Navy-Marine; Corps Memorial	Natural
Nebraska	Big Eight	Memorial Stadium	Natural
Nevada–Las Vegas	Big West	Silver Bowl	Artificial
New Mexico	WAC	University	Artifical
New Mexico State	Big West	Aggie Memorial	Natural
North Carolina	Atlantic Coast	Kenan Stadium	Natural
North Carolina State	Atlantic Coast	Carter-Finley Stadium	Natural
Northern Illinois	Independent	Huskie	Artificial
Northwestern	Big Ten	Dyche	Artificial
Notre Dame	Independent	Notre Dame Stadium	Natural
Ohio State	Big Ten	Ohio Stadium	Artificial
Ohio U.	Mid-American	Peden	Natural
Oklahoma	Big Eight	Owen Field	Artificial
Oklahoma State	Big Eight	Lewis Stadium	Artificial
Oregon	Pacific Ten	Autzen	Artificial
Oregon State	Pacific Ten	Parker	Artificial
Pacific	Big West	Memorial	Natural
Penn State	Independent	Beaver	Natural
Pittsburgh	Independent	Pitt	Artificial
Purdue	Big Ten	Ross-Ade	Natural
Rice	Southwest	Rice	Artificial
Rutgers	Independent	Rutgers; Giants	Natural; Artificial
San Diego State	WAC	Murphy	Natural
San Jose State	Big West	Spartan	Natural
South Carolina	Independent	Williams-Brice	Natural
Southern California	Pacific Ten	Los Angeles Coliseum	Natural

TABLE 2.13 *(Cont.)*

School	Conference	Stadium	Playing Surface
Southern Methodist	Southwestern	Ownby Stadium	Artificial
Southern Mississippi	Independent	Roberts	Natural
Southwestern Louisiana	Independent	Cajun Field	Natural
Stanford	Pacific Ten	Stanford Stadium	Natural
Syracuse	Independent	Carrier Dome	Artificial
Temple	Independent	Veterans	Artificial
Tennessee	Southeastern	Neyland Stadium	Artificial
Texas	Southwest	Memorial Stadium	Natural
Texas A & M	Southwest	Kyle Field	Artificial
Texas Christian	Southwest	Carter	Artificial
Texas–El Paso	Western Athletic	Sun Bowl	Artificial
Texas Tech	Southwest	Jones Stadium	Artificial
Toledo	Mid-American	Glass Bowl	Artificial
Tulane	Independent	Superdome	Artificial
Tulsa	Missouri Valley	Skelly	Artificial
UCLA	Pacific Ten	Rose Bowl	Natural
Utah	WAC	Rice	Artificial
Utah State	Big West	Romney	Natural
Vanderbilt	Southeastern	Vanderbilt	Artificial
Virginia	Atlantic Coast	Scott Stadium	Artificial
Virginia Tech	Independent	Lane	Natural
Wake Forest	Atlantic Coast	Grove Stadium	Natural
Washington	Pacific Ten	Husky Stadium	Artificial
Washington State	Pacific Ten	Martin	Artificial
West Virginia	Independent	Mountaineer Field	Artificial
Western Michigan	Mid-American	Waldo	Artificial
Wisconsin	Big Ten	Camp Randall Stadium	Artificial
Wyoming	WAC	War Memorial Stadium	Natural

TABLE 2.14: FINAL 1990 COLLEGE FOOTBALL SEASON
(Including Bowl Games)

Rank	Team	Power Rating	Home Field Advantage
1.	Miami	142.6	2.4
2.	Washington	140.9	1.4
3.	Florida St.	133.4	1.2
4.	Colorado	132.3	0.9
5.	Georgia Tech	131.3	0.3
6.	Oklahoma	131.3	1.8
7.	Virginia	130.5	0.0
8.	Clemson	130.5	3.6
9.	Michigan	129.0	−0.6
10.	Florida	128.5	4.9
11.	Texas A&M	127.7	4.6
12.	Texas	127.4	0.5
13.	Iowa	127.1	1.0
14.	Notre Dame	126.7	2.3
15.	Tennessee	125.6	2.5
16.	Houston	125.0	3.0
17.	Penn State	124.1	0.9
18.	Ohio State	122.9	−1.5
19.	N. C. State	122.8	3.3
20.	B.Y.U.	121.8	5.3
21.	Nebraska	121.8	4.4
22.	Syracuse	121.2	−1.7
23.	Mich. State	120.8	1.7
24.	U.S.C.	120.3	−1.0
25.	Va. Tech	119.6	2.1

THREE

BASKETBALL

BASKETBALL NBA & COLLEGE

BASKETBALL PARLAYS—*(Over the Counter)*
2 TEAMS ....PAYS............ 13 to 5
3 TEAMS ....PAYS............ 6 to 1
4 TEAMS ....PAYS............ 10 to 1
5 TEAMS ....PAYS............ 20 to 1

In the event of a tie, a two team parlay becomes a straight bet. A tie in a three or more team parlay reduces the parlay to the next lowest betting bracket. Thus, a four team parlay becomes a three team parlay, etc.

BASKETBALL TEASERS—*(Over the Counter)*

		4 points
2 TEAMS ....PAYS............		5 to 6
3 TEAMS ....PAYS............		3 to 2
4 TEAMS ....PAYS............		2 to 1
5 TEAMS ....PAYS............		7 to 2
6 TEAMS ....PAYS............		5 to 1

In the event of a tie, a two team teaser constitutes "NO ACTION." (ALL money wagered will be refunded.) A tie in a three or more team teaser reduces the teaser to the next lowest betting bracket. Thus, a three team teaser with a tie becomes a two team teaser, etc.

Basketball was the creation of Yankee ingenuity. A simple game developed by a thirty-year-old member of the faculty of the School for Christian Workers in Springfield, Massachusetts— later to become known as Springfield College—who, in 1891, developed a new game to get his class through the winter. It was a pastime to take the place of gymnastics, which, frankly, "bored the young men to death after a successful fall of football," a game based on the Canadian sport of Duck on a Rock. The goals were peach baskets and players' positions were dictated by lacrosse. The game was "box ball," or, as it soon became known, basket ball—two words then—and the young faculty member's name was James Naismith.

Over the next forty years, the evolution of the game took many turns. There was the surrealistic quality of playing games inside protective cages of chicken wire in armories and dance halls (hence the term "cagers") in the New York and Philadelphia areas. There were company-sponsored teams that looked almost as if they were wearing sandwich boards to advertise the company's wares: the Indianapolis Kautskys, the Washington Palace Five, the Chicago American Gears, the Cleveland Rosenblums, the Toledo Jeeps, the Flint Dows, the Warren Penn Oilers, and the Anderson Duffy Packers. These were the early members of the NBL, a running, dribbling, jumping Yellow Pages in a professional industrial league formed in the late 1930s by three corporate giants: Goodyear, Firestone, and General Electric.

In a day when the journals of record still considered baseball king and anything else was either horse racing or boxing, basketball was still a second-class citizen, generating as much interest as mutual bonds during that Depression era. But then a young sportswriter for the *New York World-Telegram* and parttime publicity man for the New York football Giants, Ned Irish, served as witting catalyst to bring the game front and center court. Assigned to cover a game between CCNY and Manhattan College, two of the many New York schools that had built up a basketball following in the winter of 1934, Irish arrived late at the closetlike Manhattan gymnasium. Greeted by a packed house and "no room at the inn" for latecomers, the resourceful Irish squeezed himself through a small gym window, ripping his trousers in the process.

In later years even Irish failed to recollect the outcome of that contest. That was relatively unimportant, but the experience led him to believe that "college basketball had to leave the gym." With this conviction, Irish set out on a bold gamble. Quitting his job with the paper, he approached Madison Square Garden with an idea: he would rent out the famed amphitheater for a college basketball game. Facing many a dark night during those bleak Depression days, Garden management was more than receptive to his idea and willing to take the gamble. Willing to risk the $4,000 rent money against a larger percentage of the gross, they let Irish have the arena without putting up a cent. If his idea failed, Irish would forfeit his option to promote more games at the Garden.

With his promotional future at stake, Irish decided to try yet another idea. He would couple two college bsaketball games, offering the fans three hours of entertainment instead of the normal hour and a half. And, not incidentally, with four teams playing, he would have four student bodies and their alumni to draw from, thus doubling his potential at the gate.

The biggest sporting attraction in the New York area at the time was the Army–Notre Dame football game, played every year before capacity crowds in Yankee Stadium. If the Fighting Irish were such a draw in football, reasoned Irish, why not basketball as well? So he signed Notre Dame. And their competition? The strongest team in the New York area, New York University. The second game would pit St. John's University, another local favorite, against Westminster College of Pennsylvania.

But would college basketball draw? That question was answered resoundingly in the affirmative on the night of December 29, 1934, as 16,180 fans crowded into the Garden to see NYU beat Notre Dame 25–18 and Westminster administer a beating to St. John's, 37–33.

Basketball was off the breadlines. It had made the leap from Off-Broadway to the Great White Way in one bounce, becoming a major-league sport overnight. Ned Irish and Madison Square Garden were quick to follow through. In eight doubleheaders that first season, they attracted 99,528 Depression-era fans, with attendance averaging 12,441, more than two-thirds of capacity and almost one and a half times as many as the Garden's supposed "bread-and-butter" sport, boxing.

The timing was perfect, for it was at just this time that another development took place that would assure basketball major-league status, not just as a spectator sport, but as a betting sport: Bill Hecht introduced the single-number point spread.

Until this time, like football, the outcome of a basketball contest was highly predictable—too predictable, in fact, for the bookmakers to profit from it. They had been quick to adopt Hecht's original two-number lines in the early twenties (Yale 13–15 over Harvard), but whereas these had proved popular in football, not so in basketball. Too many games fell on "the bookie's number," and this was not good for business. All too often tight games were won by a single point, a thought not wasted on the oddsmakers. After being burned once or twice, many punters stopped coming around during the basketball season.

A popular story of the period best illustrates the bookmakers' predicament. It revolves around a bookie we'll call Sid, who had soured his clientele with too many of these games that fell between the cracks. One day Sid fell ill. Two of his customers, Bernie and Al, met on the street and got to talking.

"How's old Sid?" asked Bernie. "He owes me ten bucks."

"I hope he croaks," Al replied. "I owe him twenty."

Bernie offered to call the hospital to check on Sid's progress. "How's he doing?" Al asked when he hung up.

"Sitting pretty," Bernie replied. "His temperature's 103–105."

At just about the same time that Ned Irish was inventing the basketball doubleheader, Hecht was perfecting the point spread. Right around the New Year of 1935 he began to quote a single-number line that eliminated the bookie's number.

Irish would introduce the National Invitational Tournament into Madison Square Garden in 1938 and, like Mary's little lamb, another tourney was sure to follow: the NCAA's started up the next year. The gate was open; basketball was out of the cage and ready to go big time.

But the professional game was another matter. At about the time of Irish's modest experiment, pro basketball still continued to hide its light under a promotional bushel. The cast of characters still featured such names as the Ft. Wayne Zollner Pistons and the Kankakee Gallagher Trojans, mere extensions of a corporate or product name, like matchbooks in short pants. The pro game languished, stunted by its umbilicus to company teams, small towns, and unknown talent. For the remainder of the '30s and most of the '40s its two leagues, the National Basketball League and the Basketball Association of America, looked like a dock walloper's shape-up. Their rosters resembled nothing so much as a bus schedule, so frequently did franchises come and go. Of the eleven teams in the BAA at the inaugural tip-off, four folded after the first season, one held on for three losing seasons and four staggered through four. The rival league, the NBL, was crowded to the foul line with franchises from towns known only to Messrs. Rand and McNally, with whistle-stop entries from Sheboygan, Waterloo, Tri-Cities and Anderson all aspiring to big-league status.

It was inevitable that the two warring leagues would merge, not just to save themselves but the professional game as well. It fell to super salesman Maurice Podoloff to pull it off. And he did, bringing the two leagues together under a brand new tent, the National Basketball Association. It opened for business in 1949 with Podoloff as its first commissioner. With that bold move, professional basketball began to emerge from its own ashes.

But it was still a long way from setting even a tenative foot on the major-league turf so long monopolized by baseball and soon to be joined by football. Entering the 1954–'55 season, the new league could look back and count twenty-three different franchises in eight years, the retirement of their only legitimate superstar, George Mikan, and a deterioration of the game itself.

It had become a foul-filled exercise in stalling with little emphasis on action. There wasn't enough caffeine in the world to keep the fans awake and, preferring to sleep at home, they stayed away from the NBA in droves.

In a dazzling feat of creative vision, Danny Biasone, the owner of the Syracuse franchise, thought he saw a solution—the 24-second clock. Podoloff and the other owners instantly sparked to the idea and it was introduced at the beginning of the 1954–'55 season. It immediately produced a speeded-up game and, even more important, more scoring. And that is what the fans wanted. Over the previous eight seasons, NBA scores had averaged 158; during the first season of the shot clock it shot up to 186. Fans at once began flocking to the arenas to see the rejuvenated game. And, not incidentally, the NBA soon landed its first television contract.

Every year thereafter, like clockwork, pro basketball added new building blocks in the form of new stars, new franchises and new rivalries, all of which sparked fan interest. In 1956 the Boston Celtics got the man they wanted, six-foot-seven Bill Russell, who had led his University of San Francisco team to 55 consecutive wins and two straight NCAA championships. With Russell, the Celtics became instant winners. In 1957 the Ft. Wayne Zollner Pistons moved to Detroit and the Rochester Royals to Cincinnati, trading in small-town identities for genuine major-league markets. In 1958 Elgin Baylor became a Minneapolis Laker, and the following year the tallest Warrior of them all, seven-foot-three Wilt Chamberlain, joined the Philadelphia franchise, immediately transforming it into a winner. In 1960 professional basketball, for the first time, became a game for all of America when the Lakers joined the westward migration of sports and moved lock, stock, and Baylor to Los Angeles. In 1960 the Chicago Bulls joined the NBA and the American Basketball League surfaced with its red-white-and-blue ball and three-point shot. After taking a breather in 1961, the restless NBA reconfigured itself again. In rapid succession the Philadelphia Warriors franchise moved to San Francisco in 1962 and the following year the Syracuse Nationals traded up to become the Philadelphia 76ers. In a single decade the NBA had transformed itself from a small-time operation into a true major league, with big-league cities, big-league rivalries, and big-league superstars.

And then, during the 1969–'70 season, basketball mania came home to where it all had started: Madison Square Garden. True, it was no longer the grimy old barn in the west forties, but a sleek new sports palace replete with a railroad in the basement; but neither were the New York Knickerbockers the perennial cellar dwellers of the early days. Under the direction of Red Holzman, the Knicks rose to the top, capping off a brilliant season with a storybook win in the seventh game of the championship series against the star-studded Lakers. Captain Willis Reed, injured early in the series and doubtful for the final game, limped to the center circle for the tip-off and scored the first Knick basket. Reed played the game in extreme pain and would not score again, but his gritty performance inspired his underdog mates to play the game of their lives. After the early moments, the clock already had run out on the Lakers. It is from this moment that many fans date the true arrival of the NBA.

The pro game enjoyed continued popularity throughout the decade of the seventies, capped off by a singular concurrence of events. In 1979 the NBA signed a lucrative new television contract with CBS, guaranteeing its future as a prime-time major league. That same year, the NCAA Tournament showcased the talents of two of the college game's most promising newcomers ever: led by Earvin "Magic" Johnson, Michigan State beat Larry Bird's Indiana State team, 75–64, in the final. Then they passed into pro ball together and it would never be the same again. With Bird in Boston and Magic on the coast, a new rivalry was born. The Celtics and the Lakers dominated the following decade much the same way as the rivalry of the Bill Russell Celtics and the Wilt Chamberlain Warriors had fueled the sixties. But now, courtesy of CBS-TV, they had national exposure.

With the coming in 1984 of Michael Jordan, with his tuning-fork hands and helicopter feet, and the rescue from the military of the promising young giant David Robinson, the rise of the Isiah Thomas–led Pistons, and its prime-time TV Nielsens, it would not be wrong to call professional basketball the sport of the eighties and, perhaps, the nineties.

Throughout the years, the college game had not been quiescent. From the early days of Ned Irish's first double-headers, the game had grown apace. The economies of scale offered by the hardwood game soon gave rise to independent giants like Chicago's DePaul who, unable to compete in big-time football, could build nationally ranked basketball squads virtually overnight. The inspired coaching of the likes of Joe Lapchick and Clair Bee foreshadowed the dynasties of Adolph Rupp at Kentucky, John Wooden at UCLA, and Dean Smith at North Carolina. The feats of such innovative players like Hank Luisetti, with his one-hand set shot, brilliant ball handlers like Bob Cousy and Oscar Robertson, and legendary giants like Lou Alcindor and Bill Walton quickly brought the game out of its peach-basket days. First the center jump after every basket disappeared; then they started taking the ball out of bounds rather than interrupting the flow of the game for another foul shot; then came the shot clock and the three-point basket.

As the game grew, so did its tournaments. Starting with Ned Irish's National Invitational Tourney, they had proliferated. Unlike other team sports, basketball lends itself comfortably to the tourney format. There were pre-season tournaments and post-season tournaments and holiday tournaments and league-championship tournaments, single-elimination and double-elimination and round-robin tournaments. Gradually, however, one began to emerge as preeminent: the little sister to Ned Irish's NIT, the NCAA Tournament.

It all started back in 1939, when eight schools were invited to compete in the newly minted NCAA. Oregon beat Ohio State 46–33 to take that first championship, but the victory was largely Pyrrhic. A movable feast, the tournament was in direct competition with the NIT for its participants, as it would be for many years. In the beginning, the NIT often provided the better lineup, although it occasionally was eclipsed by the NCAA. In both cases, the quality of the tournament was watered down by the competition between the two for its entries. One year, 1950, CCNY not only appeared in both tourneys, it won both, beating Bradley in the finals each time. It was only in the late fifties and early sixties that the NCAA began to emerge as preeminent, the one tournament that yearly crowns the college champion. It is this national championship—something that has eluded college football—that has given the NCAA Tournament the enormous appeal it now enjoys, sharing its position only with the World Series and the Super Bowl as a fan attraction—and a betting event.

The one-time "City Game," played by kids in alleys and schoolyards, had come from way back in the pack to join baseball and football in a kind of holy trinity of sports. And along the way, the game had changed. It started right after Dr. Naismith hung up the first peach baskets: they ripped the bottom out of the basket so they could get the ball back quicker for the center jump. Then someone said, "Let's just take the ball out of bounds. That'll be quicker." So they did.

And that's been the history of the game—constant change. But that also has made it tough on the handicapper; just as the game began to make sense, something new was added and it was back to the drawing board. But it shouldn't have been so. Whether it was a turn-of-the-century earthling tossing the ball up with a classy two-hand set shot or Michael Jordan airing it out high above the rim, the object of the game has remained the same—get the ball in the basket; high score wins.

The gravity-defying feats of Mr. Jordan to the contrary, the game still bears a startling resemblance to its ancestral beginnings. There have been changes to be sure, but they are suspended like fruit in Jell-O, easy enough for all to see and analyze—the three-point shot, the shot clock, the lengthening of the schedule, the coming of the playoffs. But the results are like the girl in a one-piece bathing suit: no matter how many times she pulls it up at the top and down at the bottom, it still comes out the same place. And no matter what changes have been made over the years to Dr. Naismith's little wintertime diversion, the game remains essentially the same.

If it is still basically the same, why then, despite its popularity, has the game—or at least the pro game—proved so difficult to handicap? No less an expert than Mort Olshan, publisher of the *Gold Sheet*, says, "It is generally conceded that pro basketball is the most challenging sport to bet, because so many of the games are decided in the final two minutes. Because of the long, arduous 82-game schedule, players tend to pace themselves, thus the psychology of scheduling plays a crucial role."

On the other side of the ledger we find the legendary oddsmaker Ed Curd, a man who started betting basketball right after the First World War. "The game has changed," he says, "but the final results haven't. I haven't changed my method over the years."

Why this huge gap in opinions between such knowledgable sources? The answer, my friends, is written in the thumbnail history we have just traced. Although the game has been around for nearly a century, its prominence as a TV/spectator sport is of very recent vintage, so there has been little time to accumulate a body of data for betting purposes. This, coupled with the rules changes that seem to arrive with the regularity of the autumnal equinox, has created an aura of mystery surrounding the handicapping of basketball. Because I believe, as Ed Curd does, that the winner is always the team with the most points, I shall try to demystify it.

One other factor must be considered: Basketball is a game of numbers. By that I mean small numbers leveraging big numbers. Squads are small, schedules long. Scoring events are worth very little, but their occurrence is frequent and the final scores large. One man (a point guard, a center, a sixth man, a coach?) can have a profound effect, for good or ill, on the outcome of a game—or a season—far more so than in sports with larger squads. Because the squads are so much smaller, many more schools and owners want to gamble on going big-time with a basketball team, so there are an awful lot of games for the oddsmaker to keep track of, with the obvious potential for mistakes in the line.

Bear in mind that you, as a bettor, have no obligation to bet every game. The linemaker, on the other hand, must post a price for most games most days. And this means that basketball offers a far greater potential for profit than does pro football. "Pro football is a gamble," says one successful handicapper. "Other sports, particularly college basketball, are investments." And in recent years, basketball has become the most popular betting sport at Caesars, especially during the "March Madness" known as the NCAA Tournament. (Ironically, the action falls off dramatically when the local team, the University of Nevada at Las Vegas, is playing. By state law, the books can accept no action on a Nevada team.)

But before you jump in with both feet and eyes closed, there are some warnings that must be as strictly observed as danger signals at railroad crossings. And some ground rules that should be learned. Otherwise you'll forfeit that opportunity for profit and turn your potential for investment into a gamble.

For the purposes of this discussion, I've divided basketball handicapping into three schools: the subjective-emotional, the fundamental theory, and the technical. These choices are not arbitrary; they represent the essential approaches taken by most basketball handicappers—indeed, by most handicappers in any sport. All three have their devotees, but each is necessarily restricted to a limited point of view. Although I favor an approach that incorporates elements of all three, let's consider them one at a time:

The Subjective-Emotional School

The subjective-emotional school holds that a team's performance is connected directly to their level of emotional preparedness—in a word, adrenaline. Because the most predictable sports are college sports—and basketball is the most predictable of college sports—it's not surprising that many handicappers become armchair psychologists when it comes to college basketball.

Proponents of the subjective-emotional theory would have you believe that all you need to consider in a given contest are such factors as which team is "up" for the game and whether that "up" is because they are:

- Playing a traditional rival
- Seeking revenge
- Facing a "must-win" situation
- Pointing for this opponent
- Playing in front of the home crowd
- Hoping to look good on national TV

No doubt you can think of more.

The other side of the coin holds that some teams play with so little emotion as to require a note from home explaining their emotional absence. These teams are supposedly going through the motions without emotion because they:

- Are pointing ahead to another team or a TV game
- Are coming off a major upset win or a come-from-behind victory
- Already have clinched something—anything
- All of the above
- None of the above

All of these possible mindsets are legitimate considerations, but only in the larger context of handicapping. It puts us in mind of *Alice in Wonderland*. When she finds a bottle labeled "Drink Me," Alice follows directions without giving thought to the consequences. And pays the price. Subjective-emotional handicapping is like that—it's examining only the bottle and not its contents. Any bettor who gives so little thought to the handicapping process is just picking his own pocket; he is destined to lose.

It is in this part of the handicapping spectrum that we find that curious band of souls called "the subway alumni." These bettors are not handicappers at all, but fans, perpetual sophomores—and chronic losers—who will back Notre Dame or some other adoptive alma mater with enough faith to move a mountain. And with just as little intelligence. The fact that their darlings are taking the field is enough to declare them "up" for the game.

"Amarillo Slim" remembers his early days back in Texas when he ran a handbook operation on high school and college football games. He claims that he could see these subjective-emotional types coming and would adjust the line accordingly. Often he was able to make the line unbettable but never move the fan off his team. "You couldn't drive them away with clubs! You could move Notre Dame four points and they would still bet it!" he remembers fondly.

If you must bet on your alma mater or your hometown team, keep your bets small and look at it as the cost of rooting, because it sure ain't gambling smart. Better yet, go buy a pennant and a funny hat and lay off betting entirely.

The Fundamental School

Now let's consider the "Angles Я Us" School of Handicapping, whose followers believe that history repeats itself in neat and predictable ways. These people at least do some homework, but they stop short of any real analysis. They have distilled the world of handicapping down to a few rules of thumb to fit all situations, a sort of one-size-fits-all tailor's rack for bettors. Some of their observations fall under the heading of common sense, such as Mort Olshan's oft-repeated "Never ask a bad team or a bad coach to win for you." That's good advice. Unfortunately for these punters, however, the road to ruin is paved with less profitable maxims, such as "Bet against any NBA team on the road coming off a road win the previous night."

Most of these angles work for awhile, but that does not make them immutable laws. They may never work again. Consider the following: "Never bet on a college basketball team that is favored on the road." Sounds like good advice, but, as one astute handicapper observed, home teams almost never cover the spread in games when they are prohibitive underdogs (20 points or more). And so this angle might be altered to read: "Never give points on a road team when that team is playing a worthy opponent."

This puts me in mind of lighting a match in a dark room. It flares up in a sudden burst of light and heat, focusing all attention on itself. Then, almost as quickly as it exploded on the scene, it gutters down, rapidly becoming ineffectual as a source of both heat and light. It may continue to burn for some time, but it is no longer of any use.

Take the fundamental theory that reads: "Bet against any NBA team playing on the night immediately following a game in Denver." The very first year it was formulated it produced at an impressive 72 percent win ratio. Very promising; one could make a living betting an angle like that! But the following year it suffered burnout and fell to 54 percent, barely covering the 52.38 percent break-even point. It's like the man who receives a stock market tip and blindly bets it, despite the fact that the market has already digested the information and discounted it by the time it reaches him.

It works the same way in sports betting. Once a bettor has found what he considers a reliable new angle, the linemakers already will be on to it as well. You are continually caught in the switches. It's like walking on quicksand, the ground constantly shifting beneath you. Think about this: in the 1984 NBA playoffs, home teams won 56 percent of the time; in 1989 the home-court advantage was down to 31 percent (see Box 3.1); it rebounded to 63 percent in 1990. It would be hard to turn that into an iron-clad rule. In fact, many angles are subject to such constant revision that they may be more useful in spotting trends as part of a more comprehensive handicapping method than simply being used in and of themselves as hard and immutable precepts.

The only angle we know that has any legs at all is the "instant revenge" theory. This angle works when NBA teams face each other in back-to-back games in two different cities during the regular season. Bet the team that loses the first game to cover in the second, regardless of favoritism or home-court advantage. Simplistic as that may seem, it has been a strong angle for a

TABLE 3.1: TRAVELING CALLS:
NBA HOME-COURT ADVANTAGE
(Through the 1989–1990 Season)

Each NBA Era

	Wins	Losses	Percentage
Formative Years			
1947–1949	521	346	.601
BAA and National League Become NBA			
1950–1955	1,303	478	.732
Twenty-four-second Shot Clock			
1956–1967	2,019	1,174	.632
Expansion Years, from 10 to 18 Teams			
1968–1976	3,415	2,184	.610
Merger of NBA and ABA			
1977–Present	8,684	4,600	.654

Total Seasons	*Wins*	*Losses*	*Percentage*
44 Regular	15,942	8,862	.643
43 Playoff	713	394	.644

Home-Court Edge in Playoffs

Deciding Game:	*Wins*	*Losses*	*Percentage*
Third game	24	16	.600
Fifth game	19	8	.704
Seventh game	47	11	.810

SOURCE: *The New York Times*

number of years. It came back to earth recently and began producing 58.5 percent against the point spread, still well above the break-even mark. Then our friend Arne Lang analyzed it still further and showed how road underdogs are the best bets in instant-revenge situations. But this, dear reader, is more research than angle and thus falls into the next category: the technical school.

"Home Cookin' " or Home Court Advantage in NBA

In 43 seasons, 1947–1990, NBA home teams have won 1,109 of 1,667 playoff games—for a .665 winning percentage. During the 1991 playoffs, home teams won only 43 of 68 games, for a .632 winning percentage. But their performance versus the spread was something less than "winning," as they covered only 31 times out of the 68 games for a .471 percentage— a percentage destined to make losers out of those betting the home team.

The Technical School

The technical school is for sophisticated handicappers who understand that opportunity rarely picks a lock, it requires the right combination. The combination for the technical handicapper is found in the use of numbers to gain the edge on the oddsmakers.

Bearing in mind that basketball is a game of numbers, let's review a few more. The catalogue of constituents playing NCAA Division I basketball numbers more than 250. Throw in 27 NBA teams and you can see that there will be many opportunities to get the edge on the linemakers, who may be hard-pressed to keep abreast of nearly 300 teams. Furthermore, remember that while underdogs in the NFL who cover the point spread normally win the game outright, the point spread comes into play with greater frequency in basketball—especially in the NBA. With winning favorites failing to cover almost a quarter of the time, it means that with good research, you can pick your spots.

Two other numerical factors make basketball an attractive betting proposition: the length of the season and the point values of the scores.

The NBA season, including playoffs, stretches from November to June, with almost 1,200 games. The NFL season runs from September to December, with a handful of playoff games in

January, and even with the newly expanded schedule, offers only abut 260 games. In the NCAA, Division I teams play about 3,000 basketball games, while college football has fewer than 700 on which Vegas establishes lines. So one basketball season equals more than four football seasons.

Another important element is the typical score. In football this ranges anywhere from two points for a safety to eight points for a touchdown followed by a two-point conversion, with the most frequent scores being three points for a field goal and seven points for a touchdown and an extra point. In basketball the typical score is one point (free throw), two points (field goal or two free throws), or three points (a three-point field goal or a field goal and a free throw). The larger point value of the most typical football scores and the low frequency of scores in football dictate a wide dispersion of results. A "fluke" football score can mean as much as a 10- or 14-point turnaround. In baskets a "fluke" score normally means but a two- to four-point swing. Thus a single turnaround in football can account for more than a third of the points in an average game, while a four-point turnaround in an NBA game accounts for less than two percent of the scoring.

Before you can play, you must study all of the pluses and minuses, like a little girl studying a broken doll before trying to reconstruct it. With careful study you should be able to identify potential plays, soft spots in the oddsmaker's line. Thus, the technical school reduces the frightening odds facing the handicapper.

Some of the things you have to look for in adjusting your ratings include:

• Discount one particularly good or bad game that, because of the length of the season, might have the effect of either overstating or understating a team's true worth.
• Take note of any coaching or personnel changes, including injuries, which are more important in basketball than in football because of the smaller squad. Also, the sudden

addition of a player, such as a "franchise" player like
David Robinson at San Antonio, can have a profound impact on the team.

- What will be the effect of the age of a college team? Can
a young team gel midway through the season? Will it
prove resilient over time or fall apart under pressure?
- What is the impact of the coach?

Matchups and styles are all important, particularly in college
basketball. Some teams just have the style to play other teams
better. A good defensive team may be able to contain a high-
scoring offense and keep the score down and the point spread
in sight. Also beware of a high-scoring team with a questionable
defense when it plays other high-scoring teams.

But the most important element to consider, as in football,
is the home-court advantage—only more so in basketball. This
has been called the "Home Cooking" factor, a reference to the
fact that the visiting team is away from its own friendly envi-
rons. Unlike good wine, a basketball team doesn't travel well.
It is noteworthy that, in the 1989–'90 season, only two NBA
teams—and only three NCAA teams—had winning records on
the road, proving that basketball teams, like roosters, rarely
crow outside of their own backyards, particularly when the road
trip is a marathon route. Then there are those backyards, the
away arenas, that in many cases—especially in the college
game—are bandboxes that take on the character of snakepits,
rocking with the din and roar of hometown chauvinism. Visiting
college teams, especially younger ones, have about as much
chance of winning in these surroundings as a down-on-her-luck
palmist would have of getting business by tucking her card into
a passing coffin. And if that isn't bad enough, the officiating,
while not downright dishonest, is often questionable, as the refs
can be cowed by the hostile crowd just as much as the visiting
team can. It is almost axiomatic in college basketball that the
home team seldom gets the worst of a questionable call.

Just as there are exceptions to everything in life, there are
exceptions to the road disadvantage. First of all, there are many

times when the home-court advantage doesn't count: during vacations when the student body isn't around to harass their rivals; or when the game is played on a neutral court, as when two New York teams are playing at Madison Square Garden or two Philadelphia teams at the Palestra. Sometimes double-headers played on so-called neutral courts are not what they seem. When two rivals are playing on opposite ends of the twin bill, the stands will be packed with their fans, all as eager to root against the hated rival as they are to root for their own representatives. Then there are some schools, mostly in the Ivy League, whose student bodies have so little interest in their basketball team that they forfeit the home-court advantage.

That's about all you need to know to be a handicapper of the technical school. It probably seems like an awesome list to keep track of, and so it is. What is needed is some method for quantifying all of these considerations and keeping an updated game-to-game measurement with some way of factoring in home and away strengths. With this in mind, the technical school starts where football starts, with a structured beginning, a ready reference—in this case, a reliable Power Rating. If you've read the chapter on football handicapping, then you're already familiar with Power Ratings so you can skip ahead. If not, read on.

The Power Rating concept is simpler than it looks. It is, in fact, a simplifying tool, nothing more than a numerical evaluation of a team's ability. When two teams meet on a neutral court, then the difference between their respective Power Ratings represents what the point spread should be. The figures must be adjusted to take into account any home-court advantage, but essentially that is all there is to handicapping with power ratings. If there is a variance between the oddsmakers' line and the figure your Power Ratings say the line should be— even a small one—you may very well have found yourself a soft spot. And a bet.

Let's say the San Antonio Spurs are meeting the Boston Celtics on a neutral court, say the Los Angeles Forum. Take a look at Table 3.3, which lists George Ignatin's and Mad Max's final 1989–'90 NBA Power Ratings. The Spurs head the list with a

Power Ratings of 109.1; the Celtics are halfway down the list—
we all get old sooner or later—at 101.4. Simply subtract the
Celts' Power Ratings from the Spurs' 109.1, for a difference of
7.7. Thus, the Spurs should win by 7.7 points, and you don't
have to be a member of Mensa to see that San Antonio should
be favored by about seven. In fact, given the 7/10ths of a point,
the Spurs are a good bet at −7, while the Celts are attractive
at +8.

Now let's move our hypothetical game to the Boston Garden.

TABLE 3.3: NBA SEASON
(Includes Playoff Games Except Chicago–L.A.
Championship Series)

Rank	Team	Power Rating	Home Court Advantage
1.	Chicago	110.4	1.8
2.	L.A. Lakers	107.7	1.8
3.	Portland	106.9	2.5
4.	San Antonio	105.9	1.6
5.	Golden St.	105.0	3.7
6.	Utah	104.2	5.0
7.	Seattle	103.6	4.1
8.	Phoenix	102.9	1.8
9.	Philadelphia	101.5	1.2
10.	Minnesota	100.6	2.7
11.	Detroit	100.3	1.1
12.	Houston	100.1	1.0
13.	Boston	99.8	2.3
14.	Cleveland	99.5	2.0
15.	Indianapolis	99.3	3.4
16.	Milwaukee	98.9	2.8
17.	L.A. Clippers	98.1	1.5
18.	New York	97.9	−0.5
19.	Atlanta	97.9	2.3
20.	Orlando	97.7	2.5
21.	Sacramento	96.7	5.0
22.	Charlotte	94.9	1.4
23.	Washington	94.9	1.9
24.	Dallas	94.4	1.0
25.	Miami	94.2	2.0
26.	New Jersey	93.1	3.1
27.	Denver	91.8	3.2

With the Celtics at home on their fabled parquet, the contest takes on a distinctly different tone. We have to adjust the line to reflect this by applying both teams' Home-Court Advantage Ratings (or HEDGE). Actually it should be called the "Home Advantage-Road Disadvantage" Rating because it cuts both ways, it measures both how well a team does in its own building and how much it suffers on the road. A small HEDGE means that the team's performance is relatively unaffected by travel; a large HEDGE means that they are tigers in their own building but not on the road.

To compute the point spread we first subtract the visiting Spurs' Power Rating of 109.1 from the Celtics' 101.4 for -7.7; then we add the Celtics' 2.6 HEDGE and the Spurs' 1.5, for a net difference of 3.6. Thus, the Spurs should win in Boston Garden, but only by three points. (They should win by 11-plus points on their home court. You work it out.)

It should be apparent by now that the Power Rating method is a very powerful approach to basketball handicapping. Everything rests, however, on the accuracy of your PRATEs and their corresponding home-court adjustments. But where can you find reliable Power Ratings? *The Gold Sheet*, Mort Olshan's fine handicapping weekly, is a good source. Each week he and his staff of handicappers adjust their ratings for the NBA and all of the college teams that regularly receive action. The same goes for Bob Livingston's *Green Sheet*. Either of these publications will provide you with a ready source of reliable and continually updated Power Ratings.

Another source is no further away than the nearest newsstand. Each Tuesday during the season, *USA Today* publishes Jeff Sagarin's college ratings. Sagarin is good; so good, in fact, that when his figures differ from the Vegas numbers, they often point out soft spots in the line. Wherever you get your numbers from, it's always a good idea to check them out against Sagarin's.

Or you might want to make your own figures, starting with a reliable set of numbers. Once you have established your own figures, test them against your own observations. Don't play heavily the first few weeks of the season. Instead, let the form

TABLE 3.4: CAESARS PALACE FUTURE BOOK
Opening Odds to Win 1992 NBA Championship

	Opening Line
Chicago Bulls	7/2
Portland Trailblazers	4/1
Los Angeles Lakers	5/1
San Antonio Spurs	8/1
Detroit Pistons	8/1
Boston Celtics	10/1
Houston Rockets	12/1
Phoenix Suns	12/1
Utah Jazz	12/1
Philadelphia 76ers	22/1
Milwaukee Bucks	25/1
New York Knicks	25/1
Seattle Supersonics	35/1
Indiana Pacers	35/1
Cleveland Cavaliers	40/1
Golden State Warriors	40/1
Atlanta Hawks	40/1
Washington Bullets	75/1
Dallas Mavericks	75/1
Los Angeles Clippers	75/1
New Jersey Nets	200/1
Sacramento Kings	200/1
Charlotte Hornets	400/1
Miami Heat	400/1
Orlando Magic	500/1
Minnesota Timberwolves	500/1
Denver Nuggets	500/1

develop while you refine your figures. If they say that North Carolina should beat Virginia by eight points at home and Dean Smith's squad pulls out a close one by a single basket at the buzzer, then you must reconsider your assessment of both teams, both Power Ratings and HEDGE. Was the outcome of the game due to lapses on Carolina's part or is Virginia simply a better team than you had rated them? Perhaps your assessment of the Tarheels home-court advantage is off, or maybe UVA is a better team on the road than you had thought. Can the result be attributed to the injury or illness of a key player?

Don't be dismayed if your initial ratings are proven wrong. This is not a macho contest; even the experts make mistakes. And the best time to make them is before there is any real money on the line. Some experts never place a bet on a college game until after the New Year and never touch the NBA until the playoffs.

All of which brings us to basketball's second season, the playoffs. It was sportswriter Shirley Povich who once said, "You can see an entire basketball game in the final two minutes." Now you can see the entire season in the second season. The NBA playoffs can be summed up in three words—home-court advantage (Box 3.1) with the home team winning a preponderance of their games through the 1990 playoffs.

The college season ends with the NCAA Tournament, with 64 teams playing for the national championship. And this has led to a very interesting development: the NCAA has become an underdog's tournament. In recent years NCAA 'dogs have been covering or winning outright 60 percent of the time. With the three-point shot evening things out (see Table 3.5), especially in the early rounds, the NCAA underdog has become the best bet in basketball.

But again, I must caution you—especially those of you who would rather walk through mine fields than do your homework—you must check out all of the figures and all of the angles. Basketball is one sport where you *can* beat the oddsmakers. But only if you do your homework. Betting basketball has become a tricky undertaking. Once it was like playing the cymbals— all you needed to know was *when* to play. That is no longer sufficient, now you must know *how*.

March Madness: It's Mad Dog Time!

In years past it always seemed there was some outrageous 'dog from Princeton or Lehigh nipping at the heels of the top NCAA seed. These feisty little devils would keep it close enough for three quarters to make it look as if John Thompson or Dean Smith wouldn't be able to deliver the mail after all. They never won, but they sure put on a show. And, they covered!

TABLE 3.5: THE 3-POINT SHOT

Since it was introduced in 1987, the 3-point shot has changed the face of the college game. Here are the number of 3-point shots attempted and made over the past four years:

Year	3-Point Shots Attempted	3-Point Shots Made	Percentage	Average Points per Game
1987	18.3	7.0	38.4	21.0
1988	20.8	8.0	38.2	24.0
1989	23.6	8.9	37.6	26.7
1990	25.7	9.4	36.7	28.2

Top Ten 3-Point Shooting Teams in College Basketball

Team	Field Goal Average	Field Goals	Percentage
Princeton	460	208	45.2
Brigham Young	311	140	45.0
Western Michigan	394	177	44.9
Holy Cross	404	181	44.8
Northwestern	260	116	44.6
Monmouth	308	137	44.5
Texas Pan-American	325	143	44.0
Wisconsin–Green Bay	387	170	43.9
Northeast Louisiana	403	177	43.9
Cornell	356	156	43.8
Robert Morris	313	137	43.8

SOURCE: *The New York Times*

Armed with this knowledge, we wanted to see how far we could ride the 'dog sled in 1990. There was no Lehigh or Princeton, not even a Seton Hall; but there was Ball State and there was everybody's favorite, Loyola Marymount. Seemingly going against form, the top seeds won their first-round games; but the 'dogs were there for the long pull. The results:

Favorite covered: 20
Underdog covered: 29

Interestingly enough, the 'dog won *straight-up* 15 times. In case you're wondering why the results of only 49 games are shown instead of 63, it's simple. Two were rated "pick 'em."

Normally the home team would be considered the underdog, but, because there is no home team in the NCAA Tournament, we had to throw these games out. The other six contests involved the eventual winner, the Running Rebels of the University of Nevada at Las Vegas. Just about the only thing it is illegal to bet on in Vegas is the hometown team.

We tracked the '91 NCAAs just to see if, once again, it would be another "dog day afternoon" for the underdogs. But, alas, the first two rounds saw the favorites cover 29 times in 45 games, with UNLV off the board in two games and one game a "push." However, from the regional semis on, the 'dogs finally had their day, winning seven of the twelve "bettable" games—UNLV was in three that were not up on the board.

So, if it's 'dogs you want, 'dogs you can find. But you must know where to look. And in the 1991 NCAAs, that was only after the 64 teams had been cut down to the final eight. But they were there if you used a little patience—and a divining rod for good measure.

TABLE 3.6: 45-SECOND CLOCK AND EFFECT ON SCORING

The 45-second clock revolutionized college baskets. When it was introduced in 1986, the average college game produced 138.7 points a game. Here's how it has changed the game:

Year	Average Number of Points per Game	Points per Game	Percentage
1985	138.3		
1986	138.7	+ 0.4	+00.2
1987	145.5	+ 6.8	+ 4.9
1988	147.8	+ 2.3	+ 1.6
1989	151.4	+ 3.6	+ 2.5
1990	149.8	− 1.6	− 1.1
1985–1990		+11.5	+ 8.3

SOURCE: *USA Today*

TABLE 3.7: BASKETBALL ODD-ITIES

The NCAA basketball champion and runners-up, with their ranking (in parentheses) at the start of the tournament in the Associated Press poll.

Year	Winner (Ranking)	Runner-Up (Ranking)
1949	Kentucky (1)	Oklahoma State (2)
1950	CCNY (NR)	Bradley (1)

TABLE 3.7 (cont.)

Year	Winner (Ranking)	Runner-Up (Ranking)
1951	Kentucky (1)	Kansas State (4)
1952	Kansas (8)	St. John's (10)
1953	Indiana (1)	Kansas (3)
1954	LaSalle (2)	Bradley (7)
1955	San Francisco (1)	LaSalle (3)
1956	San Francisco (1)	Iowa (4)
1957	North Carolina (1)	Kansas (2)
1958	Kentucky (9)	Seattle (18)
1959	California (11)	West Virginia (10)
1960	Ohio State (3)	California (2)
1961	Cincinnati (2)	Ohio State (1)
1962	Cincinnati (2)	Ohio State (1)
1963	Loyola, Chicago (3)	Cincinnati (1)
1964	UCLA (1)	Duke (3)
1965	UCLA (2)	Michigan (1)
1966	Texas Western (3)	Kentucky (1)
1967	UCLA (1)	Dayton (NR)
1968	UCLA (2)	North Carolina (4)
1969	UCLA (1)	Purdue (6)
1970	UCLA (2)	Jacksonville (4)
1971	UCLA (1)	Villanova (18)
1972	UCLA (1)	Florida State (10)
1973	UCLA (1)	Memphis State (12)
1974	North Carolina State (1)	Marquette (3)
1975	UCLA (1)	Kentucky (2)
1976	Indiana (1)	Michigan (9)
1977	Marquette (7)	North Carolina (5)
1978	Kentucky (1)	Duke (7)
1979	Michigan State (3)	Indiana State (1)
1980	Louisville (2)	UCLA (NR)
1981	Indiana (9)	North Carolina (6)
1982	North Carolina (1)	Georgetown (6)
1983	North Carolina State (16)	Houston (1)
1984	Georgetown (2)	Houston (5)
1985	Villanova (NR)	Georgetown (1)
1986	Louisville (7)	Duke (1)
1987	Indiana (3)	Syracuse (10)
1988	Kansas (NR)	Oklahoma (4)
1989	Michigan (10)	Seton Hall (11)
1990	Nevada–Las Vegas (3)	Duke (12)
1991	Duke (6)	Kansas (12)

TABLE 3.8: FREE THROWS: BIG TEN VS. THE BIG EAST
IN THE NCAA's

Game	Big Ten	Big East
1980 Regional Championship	Iowa 81	Georgetown 80
1980 Regional Semifinals	Iowa 88	Syracuse 77
1980 Second Round	Purdue 87	St. John's 72
1983 Regional Semifinals	Villanova 55	Iowa 54
1983 Second Round	Ohio State 79	Syracuse 74
1984 Second Round	Illinois 64	Villanova 56
1985 Second Round	Villanova 59	Michigan 55
1986 Second Round	Michigan State 80	Georgetown 68
1987 Championship	Indiana 74	Syracuse 73
1987 Second Round	Georgetown 82	Ohio State 79
1988 Second Round	Villanova 68	Illinois 63
1989 Regional Semifinals	Seton Hall 78	Indiana 65
1989 Regional Championship	Illinois 89	Syracuse 86
1989 Championship	Michigan 80	Seton Hall 79 (OT)
1990 First Round	Ohio State 84	Providence 83 (OT)
1990 Regional Semifinals	Minnesota 82	Syracuse 75
1991 Regional Semifinals	St. John's 91	Ohio State 74

Head-to-Head Results:
Big Ten Wins: 11
Big East Wins: 5

TABLE 3.9: 1990–'91 NCAA BASKETBALL SEASON
(Includes All Championship NCAA and NIT Tournament Games)

Rank	Team	Power Rating	Home Court Advantage
1.	UNLV	126.1	0.9
2.	Duke	125.3	1.9
3.	Arkansas	125.2	2.4
4.	No. Carolina	122.3	2.2
5.	Arizona	120.2	3.8
6.	Indiana	120.1	2.6
7.	Kansas	119.5	7.3
8.	Okla. St.	119.4	3.1
9.	Seton Hall	117.1	3.7
10.	UCLA	116.7	3.6
11.	Missouri	115.4	3.3
12.	Georgetown	115.2	1.4
13.	Connecticut	114.6	1.2
14.	Syracuse	114.3	11.5
15.	Kentucky	114.3	1.8

TABLE 3.9 (cont.)

Rank	Team	Power Rating	Home Court Advantage
16.	Ohio State	114.0	2.4
17.	LSU	113.7	3.8
18.	N.C. State	113.0	2.3
19.	Nebraska	112.9	1.2
20.	Alabama	112.8	3.0
21.	Mich. State	112.8	2.9
22.	Georgia Tech	112.8	4.4
23.	Pitt	112.2	3.4
24.	USC	112.0	3.2
25.	Virginia	111.4	4.4

◆ FOUR ◆

BASEBALL

"You can look it up"
—Casey Stengel

◆ ◆ ◆

BASEBALL
Wagering on baseball is done by **laying** or **taking** money odds.
— The minus (−) on the electronic wagering display board indicates the favorite.
— The plus (+) indicates the underdog.

Example: YANKEES −150 ANGELS +135	Player would lay $150.00 to win $100.00 or $15.00 to win $10.00 on the Yankees. Player would wager $100.00 to win $135.00 or $10.00 to win $13.50 on the Angels, etc.
Example: DODGERS −115 PADRES EVEN	Player would lay $115.00 to win $100.00 or $11.50 to win $10.00 on the Dodgers. Player would wager even money or $100.00 to win $100.00 on the Padres, etc.

When the New York Mets were created out of whole cloth in 1962 they were a ragtag mixed bag of over-the-hill pros and raw rookies fresh from the campus and the minor leagues. When this concoction of the overripe and the unready assembled for spring training, their manager, the legendary Casey Stengel, regarded their opening workout with something less than ecstasy. They certainly did not call to mind his pennant-winning years with the Yankees. Their spotty skills were more reminiscent of his days as a player with the old Trolley Dodgers of Brooklyn. Having already coined the word *Amazin'* to mask their deficiencies, for once Stengel found himself almost at a loss for words—but not for long. Deciding to begin at the beginning, he called them all together and held up a ball. "Gentlemen," he said, his tongue planted firmly in his cheek, "this is a baseball."

There's nothing like starting with the basics, for you must have a strategic and tactical grasp of any sport you intend to bet or you will find yourself at a disadvantage. If you don't already know how the game is played, then you have no business reading this chapter. Uninformed wagering should bear the surgeon general's warning; it may be hazardous to your health. Unlike Stengel, I will assume that you know how the game is played so we can concentrate on the wagering aspects.

Historically baseball has been not only the National Pastime but a major source of betting action. Until the rise of professional football in the sixties it was the major attraction for the betting dollar. But that has changed. Radically. Lou D'Amico of Caesars Palace Sports Book estimates that baseball currently accounts for approximately 22 percent of the action at the Sports Book—slightly more than half that of football.

We think the situation is about to change, however. Three factors are emerging that together will rekindle the interest in baseball and make it the betting sport of the nineties:

- The explosion of television coverage
- An enormous increase in the amount and quality of information available

• The increased power and sophistication of the handicapping tools at the bettor's command

Just as television was directly responsible for the tremendous boom enjoyed by pro football during the sixties—and that incredible cultural phenomenon of "Monday Night Football" in the seventies—wall-to-wall television exposure of baseball will refuel the popularity of baseball betting. Starting with the 1990 season, ESPN carries 160 games a season, with single games on Sunday and Wednesday nights and doubleheaders on Tuesdays and Fridays. Add to this the superstations: WTBS, with about 110 Atlanta Braves games; WWOR with 75 Mets games; WGN with Chicago Cubs and White Sox games, and other local and cable outlets. It all adds up to a baseball smorgasbord. And where TV goes, so goes the action, for bettors love to be able to watch their money at work and at play.

Just as baseball has been called the most cerebral of sports, the handicapping of baseball is the most cerebral of betting activities. Up-to-date statistics on pitchers, streaks, runs scored and runs allowed are the nuggets necessary to intelligent betting. Without them the bettor is flying blind. Historically the dedicated baseball handicapper did his own record keeping. This comes as second nature to a real baseball fan, who, according to the late Arthur Daley of *The New York Times*, "has the digestive apparatus of a billy goat. He can, and does, devour any set of diamond statistics with insatiable appetite and then nuzzles for more." Because this required long hours of daily application, it was a deterrent to the majority of the betting public.

Fortunately, help is now available, as close as your local newsstand. Fresh stats can be had each and every day for just a half a dollar, the price of *USA Today*. Even in the hands of an unsophisticated bettor, new to baseball handicapping, this information can be invaluable. In addition to this daily dose of data, there are the valuable compilations of statistics that have multiplied in the past few years: Bill James's *Baseball Abstract*, *The Elias Baseball Analyst*, and their imitators. These have been encouraged by a resurgent interest in the game itself and the rise of that phenomenon, the Rotisserie League. Always information intensive, baseball is the sport of the Information Age.

Finally, record keeping and analysis don't have to be like mining coal with a nail file. New tools make it possible for the handicapper to amass more data and cross-rough it in far more useful ways than ever before. The pocket calculator and the personal computer have replaced the slide rule and the notebook as the indispensable instruments of handicapping. And we can expect to see major breakthroughs in handicapping software in the near future.

But owning a Stradivarius does not make you an instant Isaac Stern. You have to get the feel of the tools; use them and find out how they can help you to handicap one of the most complicated—and enjoyable—of sports.

There are many opportunities to bet major league baseball than any other sport. With 26 teams playing 162-game schedules, there are 2,106 games during the regular season. With the League Championships and the World Series this adds up to a lot of action. For the bettor this is both good news and bad— good because of the increase in potential betting situations; bad because of the enormous amount of data to be absorbed and digested before making a bet. And baseball, like no other sport, requires a good grasp of statistics and how they relate to the placing of a wager.

Now, don't get the wrong idea. We're not talking quantum mechanics here, but some assembly is required; a modest grasp of simple arithmetic can mean the difference between prosperity and subsistence level when betting baseball. Rather than offering an advanced course in statistical analysis, let's see if we can't cut through some of the clutter and develop a rational approach to handicapping.

First of all, let's consider the betting information available and what it means. Here's the opening line posted on the Caesars Palace Sports Book board for a National League game played on June 4, 1989:

| L.A. DODGERS | Belcher | − 105 | 7 |
| HOUSTON ASTROS | Forsch | − 110 | |

The visiting Dodgers (visitors are always listed first) are sending Tim Belcher to the mound. The home team, the Astros, is countering with Bob Forsch. The Astros opened a slight favorite in the money line at − 110, with the Dodgers right behind at − 105—which means that if you like the Dodgers, you must bet $105 to win $100; if you favor the Astros, you will wager $110 to win $100. (There is no point spread; for you to cash a bet, your team must win straight-up.) The "7" is the over/under number; as in other games, you may bet on whether the total runs scored by both teams will exceed or fall short of this number.

I must take a moment to digress here before total confusion sets in. The money line is quoted universally by Nevada bookmaking establishments, but you won't find it in your local paper. As the oldest of American spectator sports, the National Pastime is also the granddaddy of betting sports. And although any record was quickly lost in the dust kicked up by the first man to steal second, the first man-to-man bet probably was made by a couple of fans watching someone called Doubleday or Cartwright or Casey at the bat. Bookmakers were quick to follow, and by the turn of the century the popular press had caught on to the public interest in betting baseball. Enterprising journalists—no doubt bettors themselves—began quoting odds in their newspapers, in whatever form it came to them. In that day of train travel, when ideas and customs traveled more slowly, this form varied widely from region to region. A quick glance at Table 4.1 points up the fact that when they were handing out good old American ingenuity, bookies were at the front of the line. First of all, many of the prices reflect the almost universal shorthand employed by bookies in quoting only the odds on the favorite. Some are still based on the turn-of-the-century practice of quoting everything against the five-dollar bill, which at that time represented a good day's pay. (Eastern odds are framed as "5½–6½," which,

TABLE 4.1: BASEBALL LINES

Las Vegas Line	Detroit Line	Oklahoma Line	California Line	Western Line	Eastern Line
Pick	90/90	90/90	Pick	9/10	Pick
120	85	80	9½–8½	4/5	Even–6
130	80	75	8½–7½	3/4	5½–6½
140	75	70	8–7	7/10	6–7
150	70	65	7½–6½	13/20	6½–7½
160	65	60	7–6	3/5	7–8
170	60	55	6½–5½	11/20	7½–8½
180	55	50	6–5	11/20	8–9
190	50	45	5½–4½	1/2	8½–9½
200	45	40	5–4	1/2	8½–2
220	40	35	4½–3½	9/20	9–11
240	35	30	4–3	2/5	10–12
260	Runs	30	4–3	2/5	11–13
280	Runs	25	Runs	Runs	12–14

translated, means you must bet $5.50 on the favorite to win $5 and you will receive $6.50 for every $5 risked on the under-dog.)

Today, although it travels much more rapidly, custom still dies slowly and regionalisms persist. This has not made matters any easier for the would-be baseball bettor, who all too often can be found glancing distractedly back and forth between a newspaper and the odds board, his face screwed up into a fair imitation of Dick Tracy's old nemesis, Pruneface. Many give up in disgust, walking away from what might well be a pleasant and profitable pastime. Our advice, if you've a mind to make a wager on baseball, is to hang in there. First of all, the Vegas money line is by far the most flexible of all the lines because it can be graded in half steps, all numbers ending in either "5" or "0"; second, if you're having translation problems with your newspaper odds, ask one of the friendly people at Caesars for help. That's what they're there for.

Returning to our example game, let's take a look at the closing line:

L.A. DODGERS	Belcher	− 105	− 105	7
HOUSTON ASTROS	Forsch	− 110	− 110	

Nothing significant happened to alter the line and it closed as it opened, with the Astros as slight favorites. The pitchers—Belcher for the Dodgers, Forsch for the Astros—started as advertised. This is extremely important, as it is what sets a baseball bet apart from any other in the house. Pitching is considered the most important single facet of baseball handicapping—so important, in fact, that the odds on a baseball bet can change *after* you place it! Let's say the Astros' Bob Forsch slips on a cake of Life Buoy in the shower and is unable to start. Houston manager Art Howe is short of starters and has to press a little-used long reliever into service for his first start in nine years. (We'll call him John Doe.) The situation has changed radically, and the betting line must move to reflect it. The new line might look something like this:

L.A. DODGERS	Belcher	− 105	− 200	8
HOUSTON ASTROS	Doe	− 110	+ 185	

That's a dramatic move. From being a slight underdog, the Dodgers have moved to strong (2–1) favoritism and the over/under spot has been upped to eight. Ordinarily, on any bet made in the Sports Book, you would be sitting pretty, secure in the knowledge that your bet on a strong favorite had been made at a very attractive price. Unfortunately, that is not the case here. Because of the overwhelming importance placed on starting pitching, the baseball bet is the only bet in the house subject to change. If, at the time you make your wager, you specify "pitchers must go," then your bet is off when a pitching change is made. If you did *not* specify this, then your money will now be at risk at the revised price. An over/under wager is similarly affected. Of course, ordinary changes in the line, not brought about by a pitching change, will not change the bet.

The emphasis on pitching is not misplaced, for this is the single most important factor in the game of baseball handicapping and, arguably, in the game itself. It has been said—perhaps too often, but it is true—"Good pitching beats good hitting." This has always been true, but with the passage of time it becomes, if possible, even more so. The arms seem to get stronger. This is no illusion. Improved training methods and facilities, a better grasp of the science of pitching, better coaching in colleges and in the minor leagues, the development of relief specialists, and even new pitches—like the split-fingered fastball, unheard of a few years ago—combine to keep the pitchers ahead of the hitters. Organized baseball has had to resort to gimmicks, like the designated hitter, and subterfuge, like the shrinking of the strike zone, to keep the offense in the game. The linemakers are acutely aware of all of these factors, hence the anomaly of the change in the rules of sports-book betting. As the linemaker looks to the pitchers first, so shall we.

The Starting Pitcher

Throughout baseball history there have been pitchers who have only had to throw their gloves out onto the field to beat certain teams; when this happens, it is said that the pitcher "owns" them. Of New York Giant great Christy Mathewson, Damon Runyon once wrote, "Mathewson pitched against Cincinnati yesterday. Another way of putting it is that Cincinnati lost a game of baseball. The first statement means the same as the second." Over the years, others have conducted their own unique reigns of terror over given teams. Frank Lary naturally comes to mind. When he pitched for the Detroit Tigers in the fifties and early sixties, he so dominated the New York Yankees that he became known as "the Yankee Killer."

There are a few pitchers today who have abnormal success against one club. One of them is Dwight Gooden of the Mets. He loves to face the Chicago Cubs. As of June 26, 1990, Gooden boasted a 20–3 record versus the Cubbies, with one save. Here are some other "dominators." (Note that 1989 records reflect the pitcher's record in *games started* against the target clubs):

> Eric Show: 16–3 lifetime versus Atlanta
> Orel Hershiser: 13–6 lifetime versus San Francisco
> Dave Stieb: 22–4 lifetime versus the White Sox
> Dave Stewart: 13–2 lifetime versus Milwaukee
> Ted Higuera: 14–2 lifetime versus the Yankees

Boston's Roger Clemens owns three different teams. He has a combined lifetime record of 34–6 versus the Twins, Royals and Indians.

This angle can work in reverse as well. During the 1989 season, the usually dominant Orel Hershiser of the Dodgers was a combined 0–7 against the Mets and Padres.

This information is available in the pages of that indispensable handicapping aid *USA Today*.

Concentrating on the consistent work of these fine practitioners of the art of pitching is like getting money from home without writing, but these magic matchups do not come every day. In the whole of the 1989 season, Eric Show, the consistent conqueror of the Atlanta Braves, did not face them once. So, while these opportunities pop up once in awhile and we must be alert for them, we also need to be able to evaluate everyday matchups. On Tuesday, May 8, 1990, the San Francisco Giants came into Shea Stadium to meet the New York Mets. Here's what the line looked like:

SAN FRANCISCO	Reuschel	+ 130	7½
NEW YORK METS	Fernandez	− 145	

Rick Reuschel is starting for the Giants, while Sid Fernandez is pitching for the favorite, the Mets. A quick scan of the sporting press tells us that Fernandez, the Mets' most reliable pitcher during 1989, has been struggling. His record at this juncture is only 1–2, with a 3.73 Earned Run Average (ERA). His lifetime record against the Giants is only 2–3. So far, not much to lay odds on. On the other side of the ledger, Rick Reuschel, a large man well into his forties, boasts a record of 2–2 with an ERA of 4.91. Not much better than Fernandez, but throughout his

TABLE 4.2: TEAM BATTING AVERAGES VS. RIGHTIES AND VS. LEFTIES, 1990 SEASON

Team	Vs. Righties	Vs. Lefties	+/− Average
National League			
Atlanta Braves	.239	.272	+ .033
Chicago Cubs	.261	.267	+ .006
Cincinnati Reds	.257	.280	+ .023
Houston Astros	.235	.253	+ .018
Los Angeles Dodgers	.264	.258	− .006
Montreal Expos	.257	.239	− .018
New York Mets	.271	.233	− .038
Philadelphia Phillies	.256	.252	− .004
Pittsburgh Pirates	.260	.257	− .003
St. Louis Cardinals	.260	.250	− .010
San Diego Padres	.256	.261	+ .005
San Francisco Giants	.254	.276	+ .022
American League			
Baltimore Orioles	.247	.242	− .005
Boston Red Sox	.269	.280	+ .011
California Angels	.256	.270	+ .014
Chicago White Sox	.254	.265	+ .011
Cleveland Indians	.260	.285	+ .025
Detroit Tigers	.261	.253	− .008
Kansas City Royals	.265	.271	+ .006
Milwaukee Brewers	.256	.256	+/− .000
Minnesota Twins	.259	.281	+ .022
New York Yankees	.237	.250	+ .013
Oakland A's	.246	.277	+ .031
Seattle Mariners	.256	.267	+ .011
Texas Rangers	.254	.270	+ .016
Toronto Blue Jays	.271	.252	− .019

long career he has compiled a record of 14–24 against the Mets, for only a .368 percentage. A bet on Fernandez is looking better.

How important can this past record be? Isn't a pitcher's current performance more important than ancient history? When considering *team* performance, you usually can throw out past performance before the current year, but when considering *individual* performance, patterns develop that tend to hold true year in and year out. This is just as true of the second-line pitchers as it is with the stars. In Reuschel's case, the tendencies of an entire career indicate that the Mets own him, rather than the other way around. Fernandez's dismal record against the Giants—although even lower percentagewise than his opponent's—is, however, of much shorter duration and does not indicate the Giants have established mastery over him. This, coupled with a lower ERA, probably justifies the favoritism, but we still haven't enough information to make a betting decision. We must consider the respective bullpens.

The Bullpen

Back in baseball's antediluvian days, a pitching staff consisted of but two kinds of pitchers: starters and those who were not. Period. Those nonstarters were relegated to sit in the "bullpen," so-called because it was situated in the outfield beneath the Bull Durham sign, there to await the manager's call to relieve. In those days of iron men, a starter usually finished what he started, so relief appearances were few and far between.

Over time, the relief specialist began to emerge, starting with Wilcy Moore and Firpo Marberry in the '20s, "Fireman" Johnny Murphy and Mace Brown in the '30s, and Joe Page in the '40s. Gradually this has wrought a profound change in the game. Nowadays a starting pitcher seldom pitches a complete game. Nor is he expected to, particularly a power pitcher. Current wisdom calls for him to pitch all-out until he tires. If this occurs before the eighth inning they bring in a "long reliever," a man conditioned to pitch effectively for several innings. If it is late in the game and they have a lead or the game is close, the manager will bring in the ace reliever, the "closer," who will throw heat past the few remaining batters and "save" the game. True to the maxim "Good pitching will beat good hitting," with fresh arms coming at them for nine full innings, the hitters see nothing but good pitching. Or so the theory goes. Part of the task of the handicapper is to evaluate the relative merits of opposing bullpens.

As this arcane art of relief pitching has evolved over time, stating its value in precise terms has become possible only within the last few years. Won-lost records mean next to nothing; ERA is a little more useful; strikeouts and walks are very deceiving. Although the best play with runners in scoring position may be to strike out the side, it probably isn't when there's one on base. The more successful closers will usually prefer to let the opponents put the ball in play, relying on their fielders to make putouts. Conversely, with the intentional pass a tried-and-true late-inning tactic, the number of walks is a misleading statistic. The number of saves is a much more useful figure. It is awarded for protecting a lead in late innings, and that is precisely the definition of the closer's role.

Turning back to the analysis of the Giants-Mets encounter on May 8, find the records of the respective closers. San Francisco's then newly acquired Steve Bedrosian has no relief record against the Mets, but the Mets stopper, John Franco, also new with his club, has seen the Giants several times. Franco has a record of one win, one loss and three saves against San Francisco. The won-lost record is neutral, with the win canceling out the loss, but the saves add an optimistic note. It is not a large bulge but another positive indicator in the handicapping process. There are still other factors to consider.

The Home-Field Advantage

As in other sports, the ballpark is more hospitable to its regular tenants than it is to visitors, and for all of the usual reasons: the home fans, the home clubhouse, even home cooking. But, at least in a few cases, there are advantages peculiar to baseball, not the least of which is familiarity with the peculiarities of the home park. As George F. Will quotes Cal Ripken, Jr., as saying, "When Kansas City comes to Baltimore, they have to play Orioles baseball."

Most of the newer ballparks, built since the second World War, and seemingly stamped out with the same cookie cutter, are large and symmetrical in shape, affording plenty of room for outfielders to get under fly balls; in short, they are pitchers' parks. Older fields, like Wrigley Field in Chicago and Fenway Park in Boston, feature idiosyncracies that generally favor the home team.

The Red Sox have long been tough at home because the lineup is tailored to fit "the Green Monster," the towering left-field wall that stands a mere 315 feet from home plate. Foul territory is meager, with low-lying box seats slicing away at the playing field, affording a second chance to many an errant hitter. Over the years, retreaded right-handed hitters have found new life in old bats, while left-handed power pitchers have "died young."

Generations of right-handed lineups have made the Sox awesome at home and strangely inept and vulnerable on the road. Let's take a look at the record: both times the Red Sox lost the pennant to the Yankees by one game—in 1949 and in 1978—they did so because of their poor record on the road (35–42 and 40–41, respectively) not because of their home records, which were extraordinary (61–16 and 59–23). They have averaged .650 in Fenway in the pursuit of their last four pennants (1946, '67, '75, and '86).

Doubles are cheap at Fenway, with Red Sox hitters regularly leading the league in that category. Triples, on the other hand, are rare occurrences because of the intimate surroundings.

"The friendly confines of Wrigley Field" has long been a cliché in the National League. Platoons of otherwise unheralded sluggers, like Bill "Swish" Nicholson and Hank Sauer, have found the short, ivy-covered walls congenial. Of course, there have been legitimate hitting stars as well, like Ernie Banks, Billy Williams, and Hack Wilson, who holds National League single-season records for his 56 home runs and 190 runs batted (RBIs) in 1930.

When the wind blows out of the Windy City park, the ball fairly jumps off the bat; with a strong tail wind it can fly halfway to Winnetka. It is no surprise that the record for most runs scored in one game by both teams (a 26–23 victory for the Cubs over the Philadelphia Phillies in 1922) belongs to Wrigley, or that three of the four times that two teams have combined for the National League record of 11 home runs in a game it happened here. The winds of Wrigley blow hot and cold for both teams.

Of course, other ballparks, because of their configurations or visibility, offer special advantages and disadvantages for their home teams; some favor hitters, some pitchers. In 1978, for example, the Atlantic Braves scored 364 runs in 81 games at home and 236 in the same number of games on the road, a difference of 54.2 percent. That same year, the Houston Astros allowed only 254 runs in 81 games in the Astrodome while giving up 380 in 81 games on the road, a 49-percent disparity. Further to the point that the Astrodome is a pitcher's park is the fact that an Astros hitter has never won a home run or batting title, while Astros pitchers have led the league three times in strikeouts, three times in ERA, twice in saves and once in wins. And, in their 28-year history, Astro pitchers have posted more no-hitters than any other pitching staff during the same time—all, of course, at the Astrodome.

Among the newer stadiums, a few possess special features that provide some advantage to the home team. Minnesota's Hubert H. Humphrey Metrodome quickly became known as "the Homer Dome" when it opened in the mid-eighties. Unlike other stadia, the Metrodome is made of fabric and supported by air, along the lines of a tennis court bubble. Apparently, the blowers that create positive air pressure were providing extra buoyancy, "helping" the ball find the seats. After the first year, the air system was fine-tuned and the dome is no longer home to homers. It retains one other curious feature, however: it holds noise as no other stadium does, virtually amplifying the roar of the home crowd. This was demonstrated by the decibel level during the 1991 World Series, which the Twins won by winning all four games played in the Metrodome, repeating their "home sweep" in the 1987 series when they beat the Cardinals by winning every home game.

The other three games that year were played on the spacious acres of artificial turf that carpet St. Louis' Busch Stadium. When he was manager, Whitey Herzog custom tailored his Cardinal teams to fit their home park. Relying on the speed of Vince Coleman and Willie McGee and a supporting cast adept at playing hit-and-run, the slick fielding of Ozzie Smith, Jose Oquendo and Terry Pendleton, Whitey's teams won pennants three times during the eighties. A third-place finisher in 1989, they still posted a 46–35 record at home. Alas, all good things must come to an end. Free-agentry beckoned too many players and Herzog lost control in 1990, giving up the reins in July.

And then there's San Francisco's Candlestick Park. Even the home team hates playing there, not because of the field, but because of the weather. Even in high summer, the wind swirls around erratically, and its proximity to San Francisco Bay can make the temperature positively icy. Like it or not, however, the San Francisco Giants definitely enjoy an advantage at home. On their way to the 1989 National League pennant, they posted a sparkling 53–28 (.654) record in Candlestick while playing under .500 on the road. (Major league home teams won a total of 1,134 games in 1989, a .545 pace. This is right in line with the year-to-year average through 1990.)

It is not just the peculiarities of the field that contribute to the home field advantage, however. Often it has been helped along by the human hand. Jimmy Piersall remembers the day in Washington when he jumped up from the bench to run out to his position. Crossing the third base line, he tripped in the deep, wet grass in front of third base and fell flat on his face. Picking himself up, Piersall, furious, as usual, hollered at the nearby grounds crew, "The way you guys have this place fixed up, [Harmon] Killebrew can play here for the next twenty-five years!"

Doctoring the playing field is a subtle and invaluable art, seldom spotted by the fans in the grandstand or watching on TV. Take the "Go-Go" White Sox of 1959. With the likes of Jim Landis, Luis Aparicio and Nellie Fox up the middle, the ChiSox were blessed with great speed and cursed by a lack of power. To compensate for the latter deficiency, Comiskey Park groundskeepers tended the middle of the infield as carefully as a putting green in order to make the most of the Sox's superior speed and skill; they kept the grass trimmed down to a stubble and the ground as hard as asphalt. They kept the third-base paths tilted toward the pitcher's mound so that few Sox bunts would roll foul. Was it effective? Remember how many games the White Sox won in '59 by one run?

Likewise, when Richie Ashburn won his batting crown with the Phillies in 1955, he owed a lot to what the rest of the league called "Ashburn's Ridge," because of the peculiar way the foul line was raised above the rest of the infield. Before every game they played in Shibe Park that year, Cardinal manager Eddie Stanky tried to kick down the ridge with his spikes.

In 1962 the San Francisco Giants and the Los Angeles Dodgers finished the season in a flat-footed tie for first place. These Dodgers were led by Maury Wills, who had set a single-season mark of 104 stolen bases, most of them in what Giants manager Alvin Dark nicknamed "the Brickyard," Dodger Stadium. Dark called in his head groundskeeper, Matty Schwab, and asked him to neutralize Wills's speed by doctoring the basepaths. Schwab and his crew constructed what he called a "speed trap" for Wills and the other fleet-footed Dodgers. They dug up the topsoil right where the baserunner would take his lead off first base and filled the hole with a mixture of peat moss and sand, watered it well and covered it up with a thin layer of topsoil. It worked, with the Giants winning the playoff two games to one. Schwab was rewarded for his efforts with a full World Series share.

There are many subtle and devious ways the home team can influence the way the game is played in their ball yard. As a handicapper, you will not be able to know when this kind of skullduggery is afoot. It is vital, however, to recognize just how significant the home edge can be in baseball, and to factor it into your handicapping evaluations.

Natural Grass Versus Artificial Turf

Some years ago we ran across a system that suggested that:

- A good baseball team that usually plays on natural grass seems to move up dramatically when playing on a carpeted surface.

- Unsuccessful teams who play their home games on artificial turf are poor investments when they play on a natural surface.
- These rules of thumb are magnified when a poor artificial turf–based team plays a good club on grass, or when a good natural grass squad meets an unsuccessful team on the carpet.

There is solid logic behind this: good teams tend to be defensively strong up the middle, possess speed and feature good pitching, both in the starting rotation and in the bullpen; and these are precisely the properties required to play well on turf. Teams with these strengths normally will play well anywhere, especially when ground balls in the infield will get to them faster, take truer hops and allow them to start more double plays.

For example, the article mentioned above cited the two teams in the National League East who play on natural grass, the Chicago Cubs and the New York Mets. In the year studied, 1984, both teams had excelled on artificial turf: division-winning Chicago had a turf record of 26–22, while the Mets, who chased the Cubs all season long, were 27–21.

Well, we checked the Mets and Cubbies out on this angle in 1989 and it didn't hold up very well. True, the Cubs' record was outstanding at 30–18, but the Mets were just mediocre at 23–24. For good measure we checked out their counterparts in the NL West, the San Francisco Giants and the San Diego Padres. First-place San Francisco demonstrated a marked dislike for turf with a record of 19–23, while runner-up San Diego was quite respectable on carpets, at 23–18. Meanwhile, the teams that had been really bad in 1984 were merely mediocre in '89; the Phillies and the Pirates had identical records of 8–10 on turf.

It appears that this once-solid betting angle has more or less dried up as more teams become comfortable with plastic grass. Let's leave this discussion with this thought: that it is no longer necessary to consider the surface per se as a handicapping fac-

TABLE 4.3: BASEBALL STADIUMS

Team	Stadium	Playing Surface	Orientation, Home to CF	Field Dimensions					Weather Numbers
				LF	LC	CF	RC	RF	
American League									
Baltimore Orioles	Memorial Stadium	Natural	NE	309	385	405	385	309	(301) 936-1212
Boston Red Sox	Fenway Park	Natural	NE	315	379	390	380	302	(617) 936-1234
California Angels	Anaheim Stadium	Natural	E	333	386	404	386	333	(213) 554-1212
Chicago White Sox	Comiskey Park	Natural	ESE	347	375	400	375	347	(312) 976-1212
Cleveland Indians	Cleveland Stadium	Natural	ENE	320	377	400	395	320	(216) 931-1212
Detroit Tigers	Tiger Stadium	Natural	NNW	340	365	440	370	325	(313) 976-1212
Kansas City Royals	Royals Stadium	Artificial	NNE	330	385	410	385	330	(816) 471-4840
Milwaukee Brewers	Milwaukee County Stadium	Natural	SE	315	392	402	392	315	(414) 936-1212
Minnesota Twins	Hubert H. Humphrey Metrodome	Artificial	Domed	343	385	408	367	327	Domed
New York Yankees	Yankee Stadium	Natural	NE	318	399	408	385	314	(212) 976-1212
Oakland A's	Oakland Coliseum	Natural	ENE	330	375	400	375	330	(415) 936-1212
Seattle Mariners	Kingdome	Artificial	Domed	316	357	410	357	316	Domed
Texas Rangers	Arlington Stadium	Natural	SE	330	380	400	380	330	(817) 429-2631
Toronto Blue Jays	Skydome*	Artificial	N	330	375	400	375	330	(416) 676-3066
National League									
Atlanta Braves	Braves Field	Natural	E	330	385	402	385	330	(404) 767-1784
Chicago Cubs	Wrigley Field	Natural	NNE	355	368	400	368	353	(708) 298-1413
Cincinnati Reds	Riverfront Stadium	Artificial	E	330	375	404	375	330	(513) 241-1010
Houston Astros	Astrodome	Artificial	Domed	330	378	400	378	330	Domed
Los Angeles Dodgers	Chavez Ravine	Natural	NW	330	385	400	385	330	(213) 554-1212
Montreal Expos	Exposition Stadium	Artificial	NNE	325	375	404	375	325	(514) 636-3026
New York Mets	Shea Stadium	Natural	E	338	371	410	371	338	(212) 339-5789
Philadelphia Phillies	Veterans Stadium	Artificial	NE	330	371	408	371	330	(215) 936-1212
Pittsburgh Pirates	Three River Stadium	Artificial	SE	335	375	400	375	335	(412) 936-1212
St. Louis Cardinals	Busch Stadium	Artificial	SE	330	383	414	383	330	(314) 928-1198
San Diego Padres	Jack Murphy Stadium	Natural	NE	327	370	405	370	327	(619) 289-1212
San Francisco Giants	Candlestick Park	Natural	NNE	335	365	400	365	335	(415) 936-1212

*Retractable dome.

tor. A good team will perform well on any well-maintained surface. Other home-park advantages are more telling, such as outfield contours, groundskeeping tricks, and all of the comforts of home.

Let's return to our example game, the Giants-Mets contest of May 8, 1990. Factoring in the home-field advantage adds some meat to the bare-bones handicapping decision we were considering. Friendly fans, familiar surroundings, and an opposing pitcher who is both familiar and friendly is beginning to smell like a tasty dish. Let's look for some garnish.

Recent Performance—Streaks

How are they doing lately? Both teams have been playing poorly throughout the young season, but the Mets have just won three in a row from the Astros to boost their record at home to 9–7. The Giants road record stands at 7–5, despite losing two straight in Montreal. Although both teams show a mediocre 4–6 record for their last 10 games, the Mets have a three-game win streak and the Giants a two-game losing streak. Streaks are important. Throughout the season, a successful team will experience several winning streaks of six, seven, or even more games, while seldom losing more than two or three consecutively. The reverse will be true of the losers; they will streak negatively, losing games in bunches and occasionally winning a few in a row. The alert baseball bettor will try to spot these streaks and ride them. One could have done very well backing the Cincinnati Reds at the beginning of the '90 season when they won their first nine games!

What constitutes a streak? Surely the mediocre Mets are not signaling a resurgence of their winning ways after only two "back to back" victories? Quite true. A streak is not really a streak until it reaches at least three or four games. In the case of the Mets-Giants encounter, the home team may be starting a winning streak and the visitor has lost two, a moderately positive indicator to add to our simmering stew. One more statistic remains for us to consider.

Runs Scored Versus Runs Allowed

To win baseball games, one team must score more runs than the other. That's simple enough, isn't it? What does this mean over time, however? Bill James, the Apostle of Sabermetrics, has promulgated what he calls "the Pythagorean Theorem," which he maintains establishes a direct ratio between runs scored and runs allowed and the number of games a team will win. If this sounds unpleasantly reminiscent of plane geometry as you learned it—or didn't learn it—back in high school, you're right. And I'm not going to bore you with the math, but, because the information was available in the sporting press, I gave it a try on the final records of major league teams in 1989. The results were rather disappointing, but through the exercise I found a simpler formula that seems to work better. For what it's worth, here it is:

$$(\text{Runs For/Runs Allowed}) \times 81 = \text{Total Wins}$$

Simply divide the average runs scored by the average runs allowed and multiply that figure by half the full-season schedule to get the approximate number of games the team will win. The results for the 1989 season appear in Table 4.4.

The formula seems to show greatest accuracy at the top of each division, calling Oakland on the nose and all the rest within one or two games. Its greatest failing was with the Mets—or perhaps it was *their* greatest failing—who should have finished in a flat-footed tie with the Cubs but finished six games back instead. And accuracy seems to fall off fairly quickly with the poorer teams, as it tends to overvalue them. The essential point, however, is that there is a direct correlation between a positive run ratio and a winning season.

So what does this have to do with the Giants and the Mets? After the first month of the season, the Giants have been scoring an average of 4.4 runs per game and allowing 5.2, which predicts that they will end the season at approximately 69–93; the Mets' 4.0–4.1 ratio projects out to 79–83. This indicates that both are going nowhere, so what difference does it make how many

TABLE 4.4: RUNS, 1989

	Runs For/ Runs Allowed	Projected Wins	Actual Wins
American League			
East			
Toronto	1.13	91	89
Baltimore	1.05	85	87
Boston	1.08	88	83
Milwaukee	1.05	85	81
New York	.88	71	74
Cleveland	.93	75	73
Detroit	.76	62	69
West			
Oakland	1.22	99	99
Kansas City	1.10	89	92
California	1.19	97	91
Texas	.98	79	83
Minnesota	1.00	81	80
Seattle	.96	77	73
Chicago	.91	74	69
National League			
East			
Chicago	1.13	92	93
New York	1.14	92	87
St. Louis	1.05	85	86
Montreal	1.00	81	81
Pittsburgh	.95	77	74
Philadelphia	.87	70	67
West			
San Francisco	1.16	94	92
San Diego	1.03	83	89
Houston	.98	79	86
Los Angeles	1.03	83	77
Cincinnati	.91	73	75
Atlanta	.86	70	63

games they will win in the season? Only one: it indicates that the Mets, at least on paper, are a slightly better team than the Giants at this moment in time.

When we toss this tidbit into our handicapping stew and stir vigorously, we come out with a well-cooked dish, an evaluation involving many ingredients, all well considered. Tonight, we will bet the Mets!

And we are rewarded as they—scoring their average while holding the Giants well below their average—went on to win, 4–1, behind Sid Fernandez. John Franco got the save.

It is this kind of balanced handicapping that is necessary to winnow out your selected plays. Although it involves numbers, it is not strictly mathematical. In order to demonstrate more fully just how this can work, we developed a more systematic approach, which I now offer.

Making Your Own Line

Forming your opinion as to the eventual winner is only part of the betting equation; equally important is evaluating the price. At what point does your selection become a good bet? At what point is it a bad bet? Getting good value for your money is the key to success in betting sporting events. With that in mind, Alec Mackenzie and I set out to devise a baseball rating method that would enable us to make our own line for comparison with the oddsmakers' line at Caesars. With a little tweaking here and there, we have designed a method that can be operated by anyone and takes only a few minutes each day. Best of all, it works.

We used a computer spreadsheet program to gather our data and design the system, but all you will need is a copy of *USA Today* and paper and pencil. To ease that part of the task, we offer a handy-dandy worksheet. At first glance, some of the abbreviations along the top may seem like hieroglyphics, but they will quickly become clear.

Let's take it for a spin. We're going to run a couple of games played on Wednesday, May 23, 1990, one from each league. We'll start with the game between the White Sox and the Orioles in Baltimore. The first item we come to is "Won/Lost." We enter the *difference* between games won and games lost in the appropriate box. In the case of the White Sox, who got off to a fast start and sport a record of 21–13, the figure is eight; for the

Orioles, who have been playing below .500, it is − 6, the difference between 16 wins and 22 losses:

Teams	Won/ Lost	Home/ Away	Last 10	STR	Runs F/A	Starter W/L	Starter Vs. Opp	Closer W/L	Closer Saves	Ratings Raw	Ratings Line
ᵛWhite Sox	8										
ᴴOrioles	− 6										

The next box refers to the home and road records of the two opponents. For the visiting White Sox we will use their road record. They have been compiling their brilliant record mostly at home, having only won six and lost seven on the road, for a − 1 rating. The Orioles' record at home is 8–10 for a − 2:

Teams	Won/ Lost	Home/ Away	Last 10	STR	Runs F/A	Starter W/L	Starter Vs. Opp	Closer W/L	Closer Saves	Ratings Raw	Ratings Line
ᵛWhite Sox	8	− 1									
ᴴOrioles	− 6	− 2									

The next box refers to how the rated team has done over the course of its last ten games. This, and the next item on the worksheet, are at the heart of the system, for they tell us how the team has been doing *lately*. The "Last 10" stat provides a gauge of short-term consistency: whether the team has been playing well or poorly. For the last ten, the Sox, remaining very much in contention at a 7–3 pace, rate a +4; the Orioles, at a sluggish 4–6, get a − 2:

Teams	Won/ Lost	Home/ Away	Last 10	STR	Runs F/A	Starter W/L	Starter Vs. Opp	Closer W/L	Closer Saves	Ratings Raw	Ratings Line
ᵛWhite Sox	8	− 1	4								
ᴴOrioles	− 6	− 2	− 2								

Baseball is a streaky game, so the next category, "STR," for streak, gives us a slightly different angle on recent events. This

BASEBALL WORK SHEET   Date _____

Teams	Won/ Lost	Home/ Away	Last 10	STR	Runs F/A	Starter W/L	Starter Vs Opp	Closer W/L	Closer Saves	Ratings Raw	Ratings Line
V											
H											
V											
H											
V											
H											
V											
H											
V											
H											
V											
H											
V											
H											
V											
H											
V											
H											
V											
H											
V											
H											
V											
H											

has to do with that old favorite, momentum. Like the body in motion of Newton's Second Law, a team on the move tends to continue in that direction, and the astute bettor would like to ride with them. Between these teams, however, there's not much to report along these lines. The Sox have won one and the Orioles have lost one:

Teams	Won/ Lost	Home/ Away	Last 10	STR	Runs F/A	Starter W/L	Vs. Opp	Closer W/L	Saves	Ratings Raw	Line
ᵛWhite Sox	8	−1	4	1							
ᴴOrioles	−6	−2	−2	−1							

We move on to another critical category, "Runs F/A," for "runs for and against." This is the difference between the average runs scored by the team and the average given up. In 1989, every major league team except one (the Texas Rangers) with a .500 or better record posted a positive runs-scored record. Surprisingly, however, the difference is not large; the world champion A's posted a difference of only 8/10ths of a run. For the sake of clarity, we're going to give this rating a slight boost. The visiting White Sox have been scoring runs in bunches, an average of 4.3 per game, while their opponents have been fairly tame at 3.7. The difference is only 6/10ths, but we'll drop the tenths and express it as a whole number, six. By the same token, the Orioles' anemic attack has only scored an average of 3.9 versus their opponent's 4.3 for a 4/10ths difference; they get a −4.

Teams	Won/ Lost	Home/ Away	Last 10	STR	Runs F/A	Starter W/L	Vs. Opp	Closer W/L	Saves	Ratings Raw	Line
ᵛWhite Sox	8	−1	4	1	6						
ᴴOrioles	−6	−2	−2	−1	−4						

By now a clear pattern seems to be emerging: the Orioles have a string of negative numbers, while the White Sox, with one small exception, present a positive picture. That's right, and that's essentially the way the system works. It's a method for evaluating the teams' strengths and weaknesses side by side. But we're not done; we have to rate the pitching.

Eric King will be starting for the White Sox. At this stage of the season the right-hander has posted a 2–0 record and has a career record against Baltimore of 6–1; this earns him a two and a five in the next two boxes. The Orioles are starting Dave Johnson, with a record of 3–2; he's 0–1 lifetime against Chicago.

Teams	Won/ Lost	Home/ Away	Last 10	STR	Runs F/A	Starter W/L	Starter Vs. Opp	Closer W/L	Closer Saves	Ratings Raw	Ratings Line
ᵛWhite Sox	8	−1	4	1	6	2	5				
ᴴOrioles	−6	−2	−2	−1	−4	1	−1				

Because very few starters finish what they begin nowadays, the quality of relief pitching is as important to our ratings as that of the starter. Although the latter probably will carry more weight in the linemaker's evaluation, our ratings will give at least as much importance to the closer. His records are near the right-hand side of the page. Chicago's Bobby Thigpen has posted a 1–1–9 record. In the first box he rates a zero since he has lost as many as he has won, and under "saves" he rates a nine. The Orioles' Gregg Olson's record is 0–0–2, reflecting his team's poor record. Closers don't get much work when their teams seldom have a lead to protect.

Teams	Won/ Lost	Home/ Away	Last 10	STR	Runs F/A	Starter W/L	Starter Vs. Opp	Closer W/L	Closer Saves	Ratings Raw	Ratings Line
ᵛWhite Sox	8	−1	4	1	6	2	5	0	9		
ᴴOrioles	−6	−2	−2	−1	−4	1	−1	0	2		

In totaling the ratings for the two teams, we see a pretty impressive difference of 47 points. But that's not the end of it. Our aim is to create our own line for comparison with the price Caesars is offering. We're one short step away. Simply put " − 1" in front of our final rating of 47.

Teams	Won/ Lost	Home/ Away	Last 10	STR	Runs F/A	Starter		Closer		Ratings	
						W/L	Vs. Opp	W/L	Saves	Raw	Line
ᵛWhite Sox	8	−1	4	1	6	2	5	0	9	34	−147
ᴴOrioles	−6	−2	−2	−1	−4	1	−1	0	2	−13	

Look familiar? Right—it's a money line. Except for the seven, we might be looking at odds posted at Caesars. And that's the point—we have a number representing our evaluation of how the teams match up, which we now can compare directly with the price being offered at Caesars. Our assessment indicates that the Sox would be a good bet at 5–7 (−140). In actual fact, the price on the White Sox was −105—Baltimore was favored at −110—and guess what that spells? Overlay! The Sox went on to win 6–3.

It's that simple: look for games in which your evaluation of these stats produces a line that is lower than the price on the board. You won't win them all, but you will win enough—and at attractive prices—to realize a good profit.

Prices, you say? The White Sox went off at less than even money. Does the system produce underdogs? Absolutely, plenty of them. On the same Wednesday as the White Sox–Orioles encounter, we found this one:

Teams	Won/ Lost	Home/ Away	Last 10	STR	Runs F/A	Starter		Closer		Ratings	
						W/L	Vs. Opp	W/L	Saves	Raw	Line
ᵛGiants	−9	0	0	−4	−6	0	3	7	10	7	−103
ᴴCardinals	−4	−3	2	−1	−1	−3	−1	−2	17	4	

Both teams had been struggling throughout the young season, but the Giants' pitching compared favorably with that of the Cardinals, so they emerged a slight favorite. Still, a difference in the raw ratings of only three points would hardly seem to be something to write home about, but compared with the official line, it loomed large. The price on the Giants was +130 and they won big, 6–1.

Because it produces a goodly crop of underdogs, this rating

method is highly profitable on a relatively small winning percentage. During our workout period, which covered the first two months of the 1990 season, winners were running at only a .550 clip but showed a profit of $1,645 on $100 flat bets.

The real beauty of this method is its flexibility. You can modify the rules to suit your own betting style and pocketbook. You need not play it every day. You may prefer not to play all picks or perhaps define a more restrictive selection criterion—say a difference of at least 30 points between your line and the official price. (Both the White Sox and the Giants would have qualified under those circumstances.) This would reduce the number of plays by at least two-thirds and no doubt dramatically increase the profitability per play as most plays would pay better than even odds.

You also may limit yourself to betting only underdogs. This would give you more plays than the 30-point method while maintaining a high level of profitability.

Finally, you need not run this as a system at all. After all, it is just a method for evaluating how opponents match up. You may want to incorporate it into your present handicapping technique. But play with it; modify it; find out how it best suits your own style of play.

Post-Season Play

To cite the oft-quoted wisdom of one of baseball's most revered sages, Mr. Lawrence Peter "Yogi" Berra, "It ain't over till it's over." Major league teams play 162 games over the course of six months, and when they're done, they're not. It's playoff time! The fun is just beginning.

The League Championship Series must be approached with these thoughts in mind:

- This is a whole new season, albeit a short one.
- In a short series, both teams will be playing all-out to win every game.
- The past is merely prologue, serving to illuminate the various strengths and weaknesses of the opponents.

By all means, read as much as you can leading up to the Series. This is primarily to keep tabs on injuries and other short-term information of vital importance to handicapping decisions. And watch the contenders in action on TV. As the late season grinds down, focus your attention on the contenders in all divisions. In watching, don't give too much credence to what you see on the field. The camera's eye is very limited in its ability to show you everything that is happening on the field. Furthermore, TV people are, by necessity, selective in what they put on the air, so your view of the game will not be a true one. Concentrate instead on finding out what each manager is likely to do in a given situation. Will he maneuver to get his mound ace into as many games as possible? How deeply will he dare to go into his bullpen? How does the second-line pitching compare?

You will have to adjust your handicapping techniques some, downplaying certain angles while giving more emphasis to others. The opposing teams in these matches have met twelve times during the year, so form will have been established. Handicapping each game will follow your normal routines, with the following exceptions:

- *Downplay the importance of won-lost records.* Both teams got here by different routes, but they had to be the best in their divisions to do it. How often in the past have you seen one team run away and hide during the regular season only to lose to a seemingly weaker team in the League Championship Series (Chicago Cubs versus the San Diego Padres in 1984; Detroit Tigers versus the Minnesota Twins, 1987)?
- *Underplay home and road records.* Don't concern yourself with small differences. Unless one team shows a tendency to be either monsters in their own ballpark or exceptional road warriors, assume that they will play well at home and away. Remember, in a short series, both teams need to win every game.

- *Don't overemphasize the importance of the last ten games or a streak.* You certainly want to get down on the team with the hot hand, but momentum can be overrated at this time. If one club clinched early, they would no doubt have been resting veterans in preparation for the LCS; they could afford to lose a few and may be *either* flat or fresh. Conversely, the other club might have gone all out to clinch on the last weekend and forced to win a few; they might have used up everything left in the tank *or* be loaded for bear. It can be difficult to determine, even if you have watched both teams in action down the stretch. Unless the numbers are extreme (2–8 or 9–1; Lost 5 or Won 5) these figures probably won't reflect the same factors as they would in mid-season.

So much for caveats. The areas you must concentrate on are pitching and defense. We don't mean total team errors or fielding percentage; these are probably the two most misleading stats available. Good teams make a lot of errors getting to chances other teams may simply wave bye-bye to. No, we'll concentrate on two areas we already know:

- *Analyze pitching matchups carefully.* After a season in which to establish form, we should have a firm grasp on how well a given team will do against a given pitcher, so you must employ the standard techniques of pitching analysis in the rating section.
- *Analyze runs scored to runs allowed very carefully.* This statistic tells us a great deal about *how* a team wins its games. A high Runs-Scored average indicates good offense; low Runs Allowed means good pitching and defense; together they offer a good measure of the balance between the two. As we suggested in our rating system, the best method for comparison is to subtract Runs Allowed from Runs Scored and drop the decimal point. Favor the team with the higher total or, if they are tied, prefer the one with the higher Runs-Scored average.

The World Series

The Fall Classic is the most difficult handicapping situation baseball presents, because of the lack of head-to-head information. You are now trying to determine who will be the most dominant team in baseball. These are the best of the best, and won-lost records are useless. Careful observation of the opposing managers in the League Championship Series will reward you. It's all on the line now and a firm grasp of opposing managerial style and tactics will pay off.

Since the teams have not met during the season, the usual handicapping tools will be virtually useless, but here are a few things to consider:

- Home runs and triples are more important statistics than doubles and batting average. Together they provide a much better yardstick of how strong a team is offensively.
- Prefer the team with fewer errors and more double plays. Yes, I did say errors weren't important, but we are now comparing the best of the best, from different leagues. If the numbers are close, forget it. If not, somebody has been working with mirrors.
- Team pitching is paramount. Consider the ERAs of the two staffs in relation to their league ERAs and prefer the team with the greatest difference. (Lest we forget, American League teams will always show more runs scored, courtesy of the designated hitter.) Also compare shutout totals; a big difference will point to the more dominant staff.
- Experience counts, so prefer the team that has appeared most recently in post-season play.

All of these stats will be available in *USA Today* and *Baseball Today*.

Post-Season Futures Betting

The Runs Scored versus Runs Allowed tool is a very powerful one for use not only in handicapping a single game but in handicapping a post-season series. The 1989 division winners match-up is shown on Table 4.5.

TABLE 4.5: DIVISION WINNERS, 1989

	Runs For	Runs Allowed	Rating
Oakland	4.4	3.6	8
Toronto	4.5	4.0	5
San Francisco	4.3	3.7	6
Chicago	4.3	3.8	5

As we all know, both Oakland and San Francisco won their League Championship Series four games to one and the A's went on to beat the Giants in the World Series in four games. This may be a good angle for futures betting, provided you wait at least two months into the season—until form has been established. Use the method above or the formula previously mentioned for predicting total wins.

Post-season futures can be a very risky business, but they offer an enjoyable—and potentially profitable—way to leverage a little into a lot. Lou D'Amico, Caesars' highly successful chief oddsmaker, ruefully remembers the 1987 American League pennant race. All season long, D'Amico had Detroit as the favorite. Early on, however, a kind of groundswell of Minnesota money developed. "People from Minnesota were coming up and telling us, 'Watch out for the Twins!' And they'd put their money down—tens, twenties, hundreds, thousands." When the Twins finally won it all, the Minnesota bettors came back to collect, all telling D'Amico, "We told you so." D'Amico admits that the house "must have lost thousands and thousands of dollars." Good businessman that he is, however, he points out that many winners came back to collect and stayed the week or the weekend on the house. He likens it to the ambulance that pulls up to Harrah's in Reno every time someone hits a monster jackpot on the slot machines: it pays to advertise.

It all comes down to a question of price. The year the Twins won it all, they started out at *200–1*. If you liked their chances of winning better than that, then it was a good bet.

When the Future Book opened on the 1991 season, the Chicago

Cubs were quoted at 30–1. By Opening Day, after they had spent $25 million on three free agents and instantly become the favorite to win the National League East championship, they were down to 3–1. The feeling here is that the Cubbies were a real value at 30–1, but no team is a good bet at 3–1 before the first pitch is ever thrown.

The Cubbies quickly proved that, as the wheels fell off their pennant chances. First, their Cactus League phenom, Gary Scott, who had won the third base job by hitting .366 with 15 RBIs in 29 spring training games, was told to take his .165 average to Class AAA Iowa by May 18. Then their expenditures began to turn sour as one of their high-priced free agents, pitcher Danny Jackson, went on the disabled list—not once, but twice. The rest of the pitching staff, further crippled by Rick Sutcliffe joining Jackson on the disabled list, folded up their tent and all but went home. By the All-Star break, the Cubs' pitching staff had given up the second-highest number of hits in the League, had the fewest complete games and shutouts and had the highest ERA. Gone were the manager and the pitching coach and any chance the Cubs once had of winning the National League East. Also gone were the 3–1 odds, now posted at 50–1.

TABLE 4.6: TO WIN THE 1992 WORLD SERIES

	Opening Line
Toronto Blue Jays	6/1
Oakland A's	6/1
Atlanta Braves	8/1
Los Angeles Dodgers	8/1
Minnesota Twins	10/1
Pittsburgh Pirates	10/1
Boston Red Sox	12/1
Chicago Cubs	12/1
San Francisco Giants	15/1
San Diego Padres	15/1
Chicago White Sox	15/1
Cincinnati Reds	15/1
St. Louis Cardinals	15/1
New York Mets	20/1
Detroit Tigers	20/1
Texas Rangers	20/1

TABLE 4.6: *(Cont.)*

	Opening Line
Kansas City Royals	20/1
California Angels	25/1
Milwaukee Brewers	25/1
Philadelphia Phillies	25/1
Seattle Mariners	30/1
Baltimore Orioles	50/1
New York Yankees	50/1
Montreal Expos	60/1
Houston Astros	100/1
Cleveland Indians	100/1

**Stipulation—you have action on 1992 World Series future wagers regardless of when the World Series is played in 1992.

FIVE

HOCKEY

It's a different game from all other games; it's
played on ice.
                              —Emile Francis

◆ ◆ ◆

HOCKEY
Wagering on hockey is done by **laying** or **taking** goals and money odds.
— The minus (−) on the electronic wagering display board indicates the favorite.
— The plus (+) indicates the underdog.

Example:			Player would lay ½ goal and $140.00 to
BRUINS	+½	EVEN	win $100.00 on the Kings. Player would
KINGS	−½	140	wager $100.00 and take ½ goal to win
			$100.00 on the Bruins.

Milton Berle loves to tell the tale of the punter who, after losing
ten straight bets on football and ten more on baskets, called
Lou D'Amico at Caesars Palace to find out what was going on
that night. According to Berle, D'Amico replied, "All we've got
tonight is hockey." There was silence on the other end of the
phone and then the bettor asked of no one in particular,
"Hockey? What the hell do I know about hockey?"

The fact is that hockey is, indeed, a different game from all others and most people know very little about it. Their entire knowledge can be summed up in two short thoughts: Rodney Dangerfield's line, "I went to a fight the other night and a hockey game broke out," and the name Wayne Gretzky.

With Gretzky firmly established as one of the biggest names on the sports landscape and with hockey receiving an almost disproportionate amount of space on the sporting pages and in *USA Today*, the game has just begun to prick the consciousness of the sporting public. Granted, hockey has a loyal following in the cold-weather regions of the U.S. and Canada, but elsewhere it excites about as much interest in the average sports fan as the second man to fly the Atlantic.

Nevertheless, with the arrival several years ago of Gretzky in Los Angeles, hockey has taken on new interest in Vegas sports books and offers attractive betting prospects. In order to take advantage of them, however, it's important to understand the game and its origins, how it's played, and, most of all, how the betting works.

Hockey's roots are buried in Canadian turf, as deeply concealed as those of baseball. One theory has it that the game as we know it was first played in 1855 by members of Her Majesty's Royal Canadian Rifles. To relieve the tedium of the garrison in wintertime, they played on the ice that formed behind their barracks in Kingston, Ontario. If this is true, it provided a fitting genesis for a sport that comes down to us through the succeeding century-plus as an all-Canadian exercise.

The first formal league, a four-team organization, was formed about that time in Kingston, and others soon followed, sprouting like maple leaves, first throughout Ontario, then to Montreal and other cities of Quebec, and finally across the great plains to Canada's west coast.

In 1893 hockey took a tentative but significant step toward major-league status. The governor-general of Canada, Lord Stanley, donated ten pounds to purchase a trophy that would go to the championship team at the end of the season. His ten pounds (about 48 U.S. dollars) bought a squat silver punch bowl, which would become the oldest sports trophy in North America. Originally intended to symbolize amateur hockey supremacy in Canada, the Stanley Cup, as it came to be known, took many a circuitous side step—it was tossed into a graveyard, drop-kicked into a canal, jettisoned from an automobile and stolen from its showcase—on its way to becoming emblematic of the professional game. The metamorphosis began in 1907, when the Eastern Canadian Amateur Hockey Association, admitting to the obvious, dropped the word *Amateur* from its name. Three years later the Cup was officially linked for the first time with professional hockey when the National Hockey Association awarded the trophy to its champion. Ever since, this elusive piece of silverware has stood for professional hockey's best, its champion.

By the end of the first decade of the twentieth century, two professional leagues competed for the attention of the Canadian fan: the National Hockey Association and the Canadian Hockey Association.

With only so many fans to go around, both leagues were skating on thin ice. Like the *Titanic* after it hit the iceberg, it was not a question of whether they would go under, but how soon. Just in time, the warring leagues merged under the banner of the National Hockey Association.

Peace was illusory. Outright warfare became internal bickering, as owners fought among themselves like the Sunshine Boys. Finally, in 1917, with Canada embroiled in a World War, all but one of the owners found one thing they could agree on: they wanted to freeze out the others. In order to do so, they dissolved the league and forged a new entity, the National Hockey League.

The NHL faced off with four teams that first season—the Montreal Canadiens, the Montreal Wanderers, the Ottawa Senators, and the Toronto Arenas. Six games into the season, however, the Wanderers' arena burned to the ground, leaving only three clubs to skate out the inaugural season.

The same three teams took the ice for the second season. In 1919 they were joined by the Quebec Bulldogs, who were replaced by the Hamilton Tigers in 1920. This alignment continued for four years, until 1924, when the league added two new clubs, the Montreal Maroons and the Boston Bruins, the first entry from the United States. Once it had breached the boundary, the league was committed to going international. The following year a Pittsburgh franchise was added and the Hamilton club was sold to a new group which moved it to New York.

Opening night in New York was a rousing success. The freshly named New York Americans played to a capacity crowd of over 17,000. The event simultaneously launched the NHL into the mainstream of sports and bruised the Canadian psyche. "Hockey is Canadian," one scribe wrote. "It's been a vital part of life and concern of an overwhelming number of plain Canadians for several generations."

This was the first flowering of a national possessiveness previously unwitnessed in sports. Years later, Chris Lang, writing in *Hockey Canada*, defined it well:

> This is a ripe issue, a nationalistic issue. The same issue we're going to face with Arctic oil, the Mackenzie pipeline, water, you name it. It's a question of a natural resource getting sold out. Hell, three of the companies that make hockey sticks are now owned by Americans.

What would the world have done if the Greeks had felt that way about the marathon?

For nearly two decades, the league remained in a state of flux, adding and subtracting franchises in cities ranging from Boston in the East to Chicago in the West, but none farther than a couple of hundred miles north or south of the Canadian border.

Finally the League settled into a comfortable lineup for the 1942–'43 season: the Boston Bruins and New York Rangers in the Eastern U.S., the Detroit Red Wings and Chicago Black Hawks in the Midwest, and the Montreal Canadiens and Toronto

Maple Leafs in Canada. All were cold-weather cities, all an easy rail journey away, no more than overnight. The shape of the league stayed frozen for the next quarter century.

The dramatic growth in other sports during the fifties and early sixties largely passed hockey by. The sport wasn't exactly hurting, but the status quo remained regional and parochial. The six anointed franchises boasted healthy and loyal followings for the all-Canadian teams that played in their big-city arenas, but elsewhere, at least in the United States, hockey as a spectator sport was about as popular as tossing the caber.

During this time, of course, hockey remained the warp and woof of the Canadian fabric. And little by little, it began to capture the hearts of folks living in the area along the southern side of the border. Throughout New England and westward to Michigan and Minnesota, more and more Americans began playing the game in high school and college. In town after town, where once there had been a rag-tag band of boys in hand-me-down skates slicing across a pond, there was now an organized league playing on artificial ice, and within a few years, that would be enclosed. Gradually a huge pool of future fans and players was formed, one without professional representation. Meanwhile, in Canada, amateur hockey remained the national mania.

In 1967 the NHL finally broke the ice. If it had been slow to follow the expansionist lead of baseball, basketball, and football, it was quick to play catch-up, announcing a wholesale expansion. Rather than add a franchise or two at a time, the league doubled in size overnight. New franchises in Philadelphia, Pittsburgh, St. Louis, Minnesota, San Francisco, and Los Angeles joined the existing six. Although it would be difficult to imagine the latter two as candidates for the Winter Olympics, the League sought representation in the biggest TV markets of the U.S., and these warm-weather sites, however improbable, seemed to be good fits in this regard. The pot of gold at the end of the TV rainbow somehow eluded them, however, for several reasons, not the least of which was the fact that Canada's ice-bound, warlike national sport took a long time to catch on in the balmy climes of laid-back California.

And as if the weather wasn't a formidable enough opponent in winning the favor of the American fan, the NHL proved to be its own worst enemy. In a frenzy of self-aggrandizement, it insisted on naming everything that moves for some distinguished, if unfamiliar, patron of the game. Instead of Eastern and Western Conferences, we have the Wales and Campbell Conferences. Umbilically connected to them are the Norris, Smythe, Adams, and Patrick divisions. One hopes that Sergeant Preston of the Yukon is skating in one of them, or how else will we find our way out of this trackless wilderness? The best course is to try to forget these stumbling blocks. If you enjoy the game, concentrate on the players of the present—and the odds of the future. (Let's see, Gretzky plays in Los Angeles. That's in the West, so that must be Wales. And Pittsburgh is in the East. . . .)

In the early seventies, a group of entrepreneurs set up a rival league, the World Hockey Association, with teams in several smaller cities. Laboring, as it did, in the anonymity of sports backyards, the WHA struggled financially but managed both to tap previously unrepresented fans and to develop new ones. Lacking TV revenue and forced to traverse huge tracts of western Canada, the WHA played short-handed for several years. Finally, in 1979, it bowed to the inevitable and folded. The NHL gobbled up the remnants, adding franchises in Hartford, Quebec, Winnipeg, and Edmonton, and the League, which had played with only six teams just fourteen years before, now boasted 21. More important, it had acquired the contract of the man destined to change the game: Wayne Gretzky.

Considered by *Sports Illustrated* to be "the greatest hockey player who ever lived," it is an index of Gretzky's reputation that the second-best man in his class is not in his class at all. From the time of his NHL debut during the 1979–'80 season—neatly timed to synch with the United States hockey triumph in the 1980 Olympics—with the Edmonton Oilers, he was clearly destined for stardom. Purchased from the struggling Indianapolis Racers of the WHA as a skinny seventeen-year-old, he was runner-up in scoring that first year. Over the next seven years the man they call "the Great One" led the League, averaging 191 points a year. His very presence filled arenas much like a great actor packs them in. He assaulted the goal and the record book with equal vigor, holding or sharing, at this writing, some 49 regular season, post-season, and All-Star Game records. It was as if, just when hockey's greatest stars—the Richards, the Howes, the Hulls, the Orrs, the Espositos—were skating off, along came a single player who embodied them all. In doing so, he elevated the game to the major league level, fertilizing the sport as no one person other than Babe Ruth had ever popularized a single sport.

After leading the Oilers to four Stanley Cups in five seasons, the Great One was traded to the Los Angeles Kings in 1988. Suddenly La-La Land went ga-ga for hockey. And, if L.A., as Leo Rosten once said, "is six suburbs in search of a city," the seventh—at least on weekends—is surely Las Vegas. Infatuation quickly spread from the Sunset Strip—where Kings tickets are the hottest item in town, going for as much as $1,000—to the Las Vegas Strip. And hockey became a major league betting sport overnight.

With all of this focus on Gretzky, however, it's doubtful that you can make a lot of money betting on the Kings. The linemakers are well aware of his prowess and popularity. The opportunities are likely to be more abundant elsewhere, so let's take a closer look at hockey betting.

Many bettors view hockey as an exercise played with a so's-your-old-man mentality—the players skate up and down the ice trying to smash their opponents into ever smaller and untidier pieces, teeth flying like popcorn, strewing the ice around them. But despite this leperlike treatment, the sport maintains a hold on a small but vocal segment of the population whose depth of affection far exceeds its numbers and continues to grow apace.

Hockey lines were once posted merely as an accommodation to the occasional visiting fireman from Canada and those parts of the U.S. where the thermometer registers a low opinion of the weather. But recent years have seen the migration of many fans to Las Vegas, providing a hard core of hockey enthusiasts and bettors. This is especially true since the once conventional forty-cent line has given way to a twenty-cent line, the equivalent of the 11/10 odds a bettor lays in football. What with satellite dishes and increased exposure—especially from Los Angeles, where Gretzky has become the greatest Canadian carrier since Mama Dionne—hockey has found a second home in Las Vegas.

Truth to tell, hockey basically attracts only those in the know. Many of these wise guys come from back East and know hockey the way Bo knows baseball, often better than the oddsmakers. They lurk around the sports books like foxes around chicken coops, looking for soft spots. But the average bettor, particularly from the Left Coast, not only does not understand the sport and its rich fabric, but he doesn't understand the betting lines either. We'll consider both, but first the line.

Hockey sports a dual line—the goal (or puck) line *and* an attached money line. This is, in effect, a combination line. And therein lies the problem. Confused by this dual line, the average bettor tends to turn his back and say, "I say it's broccoli and I say the hell with it," rather than attempting to cope with this unusual line as well as the welter of statistics that form the basis for making betting decisions.

Hockey betting is, in reality, a combination wager with a money line similar to baseball and a "goal" (or "puck") line incorporated that is stated in half-goal integers to determine a winner. The puck line is expressed in a manner similar to the original form of stating football and basketball odds: "½–1." Let's say the New York Rangers are playing in Philadelphia and the Flyers are favored at ½–1. If you bet Philadelphia you must lay one goal and if you bet the Rangers you receive one-half a goal. So if you bet on the Flyers and they win by one goal, you have a push and the book wins all of the Ranger bets.

The money line—laying or taking odds on which team wins—

works just like the money line bet in baseball: your team must win for you to receive the stated odds. In the example above, in which the Flyers were favored by ½ goal over the Rangers, the Philadelphia line would be −160 with New York at +140.

And then, as if the combined money line *and* puck line aren't enough action for you, there is also the total line. Similar to football and basketball's over/under line, here you try to predict how much scoring there will be. It might be expressed thus: "7½ (over/)−120/ EVEN." (The total score quoted is 7½ goals, with the over money line at −120 and the under at EVEN, translating into 6/5 odds. Michael "Roxy" Roxborough, the Las Vegas oddsmakers' oddsmaker, also quotes odds at EVEN: −110/−110, and at 11/10: EVEN/−120, so you may see the Totals bet quoted in any of three different ways.)

You have to know the teams and how they set up (rivalries, crucial late-season situations, intra-divisional games, which more times than not are played close to the vest) and the referees (do they let the teams play, or no?). Still, it's more action—almost as much as the game itself.

That's really all there is to it. Next you have to plug in your personal assessment of the teams, and then you, too, can play. An understanding of the game is required, so let's go through a few of the factors that will have a bearing on your bet. They are similar to those you have encountered in other sports, especially baseball. And, like baseball, if you do your homework you can enjoy a distinct advantage over both the oddsmakers and other Vegas punters, who are oblivious to the nuances of the game. In the words of Don Cherry, former coach of the Boston Bruins and Denver Rockies and now a TV commentator in Canada, "The only thing those people [in the Sunbelt] know about ice is when they put it in their drinks."

To successfully bet hockey, you must first understand the game, a game made up of equal parts brutality, blood, and balletic beauty. To its millions of fans the chief attraction is its constant action, an aspect of the game unrivaled in team sports. A *New York Times* writer—and clearly a fan—was once moved to enthuse, "For pep and speed and action, there's only one attraction, [and] that's hockey."

Emile Francis's observation that hockey is different because it is played on ice comes no closer to understanding the game than defining a home run, as Italian movie star Elsa Martinelli once did, as "When the ball goes where de people isn't, den dat's good." Hockey possesses nuances and meanings all its own, some patently obvious and others far subtler.

With all due respect to those who already appreciate the finer points of the game, we're going to rattle off some of the basic points. What looks like mayhem on ice is, in reality, a precision game played by six players on a team—a goalie, two defensemen and three forwards. Their object is to put the puck into the opposing team's goal while preventing it from settling in theirs.

To start the game, the referee drops the puck—a hard rubber disk that the players hit when they aren't hitting one another—into a small circle at the red line in the center of the ice, where the opposing centermen try to gain possession of it. Once they have the puck, the attacking team tries to move the puck down the ice with sticks, skates or bodies toward the opponent's goal and past the goalie for a score; the defenders try to stop them and get possession of the puck themselves.

The game is divided into three 20-minute periods, with only actual playing time counted. During the regular season, if the game is tied at the end of 60 minutes, the teams play a single five-minute "sudden death" overtime; if the score is still even after the overtime period, the tie stands. During the playoffs the teams will play as long as is necessary to resolve the tie.

The playing surface, or rink, is a 200-foot-long sheet of ice, divided in half by the red line. A blue line on each side divides the rink into an attacking zone, the neutral zone (center ice), and a defending zone. The blue lines are similar to football's line of scrimmage, with no player on an attacking team allowed to enter the attacking zone ahead of the puck and no pass from the defending zone allowed beyond the center red line. (When a pass travels the length of the ice, it is called "icing" and is brought back to the defending zone for a face-off.)

A major feature of the game is the penalties—of which there are many—called by the referee and the two linesmen. Most are caused by the constant mugging going on by God's frozen people. There are two types of penalties: the "majors," such as fighting and high sticking, for five minutes, and the "minors," such as roughing, for two. When a penalty is called, the offending player is required to sit in the penalty box for the duration of the penalty and his team is unable to replace him. Thus the non-offending team has an advantage for the duration of the penalty. This is known as a "power play," and a team's success—or lack of it—during power plays is usually a good indicator of its overall ability. How well a team plays when they are short-handed—called "penalty killing"—is another good barometer.

That's all you need to know for a basic understanding of the game. But if you wish to bet the game, the above rendition of the basic rules merely serves as table setting. After all, you can learn the basic moves in chess in a few minutes and spend a lifetime learning how to play the game well. In hockey you must be able to understand how the game's statistics reflect the play and analyze them systematically—not unlike the myriad of statistics generated by the batting of the little white pill in baseball.

Since more than 30 percent of all goals are scored while a team is short-handed—with a man in the penalty box—special teams are an important element in handicapping. The power-play effectiveness of each team as well as the penalty-killing ability of its special teams must be charted. Teams that finish at the bottom of the standings invariably are the worst penalty-killing clubs in the NHL. Thus it is essential to accurately assess both teams' power-play and penalty-killing abilities.

One of the most important—and overlooked—aspects of the power play is the "shorthanded goal." This is a score by the penalty killers during their opponent's power play. It has much the same effect as if Lady Luck had grabbed the team with the advantage by the hair and flopped them over onto their backs; it ranks right up there in devastating effect with returning an intercepted pass the length of the football field. According to Bobby Bryde, one of the top hockey handicappers around today, "Shorthanded goals are a psychological plus as well as a momentum killer." Bryde charted shorthanded goals during the 1989–'90 season and found that whenever a team scored a shorthanded goal and their opponents did not, the first team's won-lost record was 232–100, with 33 games ending in a tie. That's a winning percentage of .700 of all games that were played to a decision, a powerful edge to have going for you.

Other important statistics that must be gleaned from the daily newspapers and *USA Today* include a goalie's goal-against average (particularly against the team he'll be facing); the home-ice advantage (NHL home teams win 56 percent of the time during the regular season and 65 percent in the playoffs); back-to-back road games; three straight games on the road; overtime games (teams that played three straight overtime games in 1989–'90 were 0–5 for their next game); the revenge factor (oddsmakers always figure it into the line); intradivisional versus interdivisional games; and shots on goal (teams with the advantage of outshooting their opponents 15 or more times had a 65–30–12 record in 1989–'90).

Because the lines for odds aren't as clear-cut as football or basketball, the point spread record is well-nigh impossible to construct. Bobby Bryde recommends that you use a straight-up won-lost record for your calculations.

One thing to bear in mind about hockey lines is the fact that almost 10 percent of all NHL games end in ties—even after five minutes of overtime, most games *still* end in ties—the odds-makers, never eager to refund money (let alone on both sides of the ledger), always add the half-goal to prevent pushes.

Finally, perhaps the most important factor in hockey is its high degree of emotionalism. It rivals European football as the leader in sellouts, which means that "fan participation" is yet another factor to consider. Go to any game and try to ignore the deafening roar of the crowd. Try getting into a hockey game during the playoffs. You can't get a seat. Our East Coast hockey maven, Vinny DiMarco, puts it this way: "I've seen nonhockey fans get involved with the home team and become fans in only one game. They jump out of their seats and cheer even though they don't understand the basic rules."

Generating this kind of heat, it is no surprise, then, that there is a real advantage to home ice. Ninety-nine percent of all teams outshoot their opponents by a wider margin at home than they do on the road. Since the basic hockey truism holds that, at best, you can stop 90 percent of all shots on goal (SOG), it follows that if your team is outshot by 10 shots-on-goal per game, you will give up 80 more goals a season than you score. DiMarco offers the following example:

Quebec 1991	G	W	L	T	Goals for	SOG	Goals Against	Average per Game SOG	Goals	SOG	Opp.	SOG
Home	39	8	23	8	119	1025	169	1247	3.05	26.3	4.33	32.0
Away	38	7	26	5	106	922	176	1507	2.79	24.3	4.63	39.7
TOTALS	77	15	49	13	225	1947	345	2754	2.92	25.3	4.48	35.8

Quebec has been outshot by 807 SOG in 77 games, an average of 10.5 shots per game. Impossible to win.

Some experts counter the SOG value by asking, "How many were quality shots? How many were hard to handle?" This argument is moot, because the ratio of goals scored to SOG remains consistent year in and year out. Thus the 90 percent fielding average is a valid measuring stick, whether the shot is difficult or easy to handle.

One problem any coach or manager faces is that of maintaining his team's motivation over the course of an entire season. This is why bad teams, like Quebec, occasionally beat their betters. This is where close personal observation is paramount. Careful study and constant review on a daily basis allow you to track your team's emotional intensities and recognize when a change is coming.

Vinny DiMarco feels that you should bet the streak until it's over, because "when a *good* team has a long road or home

TABLE 5.1: GOALIES' FIELDING AVERAGES, 1990–'91 SEASON

Goalie/Team	Games	Mins.	Shots Against	Goals Against	Goals Per Game	Save Percentage	W/L Rec.
Belfour/Chi.	69*	4,127*	1,883*	170	2.47*	.9108*	43–19–7*
Beaupre/Wash.	43	2,572	1,095	113	2.64	.8968	20–18–3
Roy/Mont.	47	2,835	1,362	128	2.71	.9075	25–15–6
Moog/Bost.	47	2,844	1,307	136	2.87	.8959	25–13–9
Hrudy/LA	46	2,730	1,321	132	2.90	.9001	26–13–6
Terreri/NJ	50	2,970	1,348	144	2.91	.8932	24–21–7
Casey/Minn.	53	3,185	1,450	158	2.98	.8910	21–20–11
Riendeau/St.L.	45	2,671	1,241	134	3.01	.8920	29–9–6
Wamsley/Calg.	28	1,670	762	85	3.05	.8885	14–7–5
Joseph/St.L.	28	1,710	874	89	3.12	.8982	16–10–2
Richter/NYR	43	2,596	1,392	135	3.12	.9030	21–13–7
Hextall/Phil.	34	2,034	982	106	3.13	.8921	13–16–5
Essensa/Winn.	49	2,916	1,496	153	3.15	.8977	19–24–5
Ranford/Edm.	57	3,415	1,705	182	3.20	.8933	27–27–3
Berthiaume/LA	35	2,119	1,086	117	3.31	.8923	20–11–4
Vernon/Calg.	52	3,121	1,406	172	3.31	.8777	31–19–3
Healy/NYIs.	50	2,999	1,557	166	3.32	.8934	18–24–9
Siborkowitz/Hart	50	2,953	1,284	164	3.33	.8723	21–22–7
Malarchuk/Buf.	35	2,131	1,090	119	3.35	.8908	12–14–10
Vanbiesbrouk/NYR	38	2,257	1,154	126	3.35	.8908	15–18–6
Puppa/Buff	35	2,092	1,029	118	3.38	.8853	15–11–6
Gamble/Vanc.	41	2,433	1,156	140	3.45	.8789	16–16–6
Chevraldae/Det.	60	3,615	1,716	214*	3.55	.8753	30–26–5
Burke/NJ	31	1,870	875	112	3.59	.8720	8–12–8
Barrasso/Pitt.	46	2,754	1,579	165	3.59	.8955	27–16–3
Hackett/NYIs.	25	1,508	741	91	3.62	.8772	5–18–1
Lemelin/Bos.	30	1,829	841	111	3.64	.8680	17–10–3
Liut/Wash.	31	1,834	786	114	3.73	.8550	13–16–3
Ing/Tor.	52	3,126	1,716	200	3.84	.8834	16–29*–8
McLean/Vanc.	33	1,969	983	131	3.99	.8671	10–23–3
Tugnutt/Que.	52	3,145	1,853	212	4.04	.8856	12–29*–10

*Led league
SOURCE: Vinny DeMarco

winning streak ended, you should bet them to keep losing for at least three or four games." The reverse, however, is true of bad teams: after a long losing streak and a lone win, they can be expected to revert quickly to form and resume their losing ways.

During a long, grueling season in a game so dependent on intensity, even a good team can be expected to hit an occasional fallow period. SOG will fall off and, consequently, so will scoring. DiMarco feels that this is a time to bet against them—up to four games—because, although they will continue to win, they will only do what they have to do to win and will fail to cover. Bets on the underside of the totals are called for as well.

Here are Vinny DiMarco's rules for betting hockey:

1. You must recognize the lull period, or better yet, keep your own personal records of home and away records of the teams you like to bet on.
2. Bad teams can get up for a particular rival during the season—for instance, the New York Islanders versus the New York Rangers. The Rangers spent most of the 1990–'91 season in first place while the Islanders languished in last place, and yet the Rangers' record against the Isles was dismal:

G	W	L	T	Goals	SOG	Goals Against	Opp. SOG
7	2	4	1	22	211	22	206

   The reason behind the Isles' success against the Rangers is that they had "no future." Early on it became apparent that they were not going to the playoffs, so their own "playoff" intensity became focused on the Rangers. This is not at all unusual for a bad team to concentrate on a particular opponent who, themselves playoff bound, is not similarly motivated. Under the circumstances, the bad team can be expected to play its best hockey of the year against that opponent.
3. Watch for the "End of the Year Free-for-all." This could be called the "All Bets Are Off Syndrome," because fully

95 percent of all streaks come to an end during the last ten games of the season. DiMarco cites the following instances from the end of the 1990–'91 season:

- Pittsburgh won 5 of 6 on the road to improve from 11–19–3 to 16–20–3.
- Pittsburgh lost at home for the first time in 16 games.
- Washington won 4 in a row on the road to improve from 12–21–3 to 16–21–3.
- The New York Rangers went on a 9-game losing streak.
- The Philadelphia Flyers lost 5 out of 6.
- The Hartford Whalers lost 4 in a row.
- The St. Louis Blues lost 3 out of 4 home games after going undefeated in 11.
- St. Louis won 4 in a row on the road.
- The Minnesota North Stars won 5 in a row at home to go from 13–14 to 18–14.
- Detroit won 3 out of 4 on the road to improve from 5–21 to 8–22.

4. You very seldom see a hockey team steamroll into the playoffs with a long winning streak. The reason, once again, is emotion. Players and coaches alike play the regular season with the playoffs in mind. You might think that the playoff incentive will help a good team play better at year's end, but it doesn't. The players try too hard, attempting to extend their game beyond their capabilities. This causes them to involuntarily "freeze up."

Conversely, non-playoff teams are all "playing loose." With nothing to lose—and next year's salary to play for—they become giant killers, taking things as they come and often excelling.

But this is a short-term situation. In general, the longer the game, the longer the series, the longer the season, the more the better teams will prevail. Tracking a team's performance and noting its emotional state is the key to winning hockey bets; it is the only edge.

There is an old saying: "No pain, no gain." You must be willing to study and put in the time keeping all home and away records, including shots on goal, rivalries, division games, and streaks.

5. Remember, if you give goals, your spot will amount to a large percentage of the total score. For example, Montreal beats Toronto at home, 1–0. If you bet Montreal and spotted goals, you lost your bet regardless of the fact that they won the game. This is a good deal different from spotting points in football or basketball, where a single score can yield more than a single point. Here you would have spotted 200 percent of the final score. This becomes increasingly true as scoring is on the decline in the NHL.

Despite the statistics to be absorbed, the different considerations to be made in the line and the choices you have, hockey can be a rewarding sport to bet. Mainly because, with homework, you may well know more than the oddsmakers—injuries, power-play potential, penalty killing abilities, goals scored against particular goalies, and so on. Always bear in mind that you have one big advantage over the oddsmaker: you can concentrate your efforts on a single game, while he must handicap them all. Of course, this is true of all betting sports, but hockey, because of its relative newness, offers more opportunities than others.

But even after all that, hockey can be a heartbreaker, with its own "tough beats," often because of empty-net goals. In this time-honored strategy, a losing coach pulls his goalie in favor of putting an extra skater on the ice. This works only about seven percent of the time and backfires more than a third of the time, when the opponent scores a cheap goal, but it always seems to happen just when you thought the game was iced.

But still, hockey is worth it. If you know your facts cold.

SIX

BOXING

The race is not always to the swift, nor the battle
to the strong . . . but that's the way to bet.
—Damon Runyon

BOXING

Wagering on boxing is done by **laying** or **taking** money odds.
— The minus (−) on the electronic wagering display board
   indicates the favorite.
— The plus (+) indicates the underdog.

Example:

SUGAR RAY LEONARD	300
THOMAS "HIT MAN" HEARNS	+ 200

Player must lay $300.00 to win $100.00 or $30.00 to win $10.00 on
Leonard, who is a 3 to 1 favorite. Player would wager $100.00 to win
$200.00 or $10.00 to win $20.00 on Hearns, etc.

Example:

MARVELOUS MARVIN HAGLER	− 120
SUGAR RAY LEONARD	− 120

Player would wager $120.00 to win $100.00 or $12.00 to win $10.00
on either fighter in this "PICK EM" fight.

SPECIAL BOXING RULES

In the event of a draw, monies on the fight itself will be refunded.
However, specific fight propositions must come as stated, such as a
draw, either fighter by knockout or decision or specific round
knockout etc. Rounds propositions will be governed by the rules
posted on our house wagering sheets and electronic display boards.

In the event that one or both fighters do not make the required
weight but the bout goes on, the following stipulations will apply:

When the bell sounds to begin the first round, the bout will be
considered official for betting purposes, regardless of the scheduled
length or title. The bout must have the original scheduled length to
have action on rounds propositions.

Boxing and betting have been an item since the days when men were men and women were damned glad of it—almost since the time when Father Adam was dispossessed by the apple stampede.

Common wisdom, which is always an underdog at the betting window, has it that boxing as we know it can be traced back to olde Jim Figg's Boxing and Fencing School, established in London back in 1719. In those days of bareknuckle fights and bear holds, the sport soon was adopted by English "sports" and "the fancy," privileged men of leisure who attended matches with the intention of supporting their favorite with a few bob. Sports of different minds would agree on a grubstake holder who would unfurl his handkerchief and place it at ringside. The punters would then place their bets on the edge of the handkerchief pointing to the corner of their chosen warrior. Another handkerchief might be placed alongside to hold "first blood" money, as in which pugilist would be first to draw blood.

Since those halcyon days B.C.—Before Corbett—Figg's rude establishment has been replaced by the Marquis of Queensberry Rules, bareknuckles by gloves, and handkerchiefs by sophisticated electronic odds boards. But the action among the sports still goes on, the same indulgences allowed in the natural evolution of time and man. This time around, however, the house has become the grubstake holder; and instead of taking wagers on "first blood," the oddsmakers have substituted the "go-no go" bet, allowing the bettor to wager on whether or not a bout will go past a certain round—or time in a round.

Almost from the moment boxing reached the shores of America, it became associated in the public consciousness with Madison Square Garden. The New York punch palace became the Mecca of Boxing, where all four corners of the boxing world met. And, over the next eight decades, the Garden hosted more than 5,000 fights, many of them all-time classics of the ring.

Beginning with the Gene Fullmer–Sugar Ray Robinson middleweight championship fight in 1961, however, the boxing landscape began to change, imperceptibly at first, but change nevertheless. Following that fight, other championships began to trickle into Las Vegas. In 1962, Carlos Ortiz and Joe Brown fought there for the lightweight title, and the following year Sonny Liston claimed the heavyweight crown from Floyd Patterson.

In the seventies the trickle turned into Niagara as championship bout after championship bout went to Vegas. A couple of unforeseen circumstances brought this about. The first was the general state of boxing. By the early sixties, the sport had fallen on hard times. Its champions were either has-beens or never-wases. The only recognizable name in the lot was Archie Moore, who by this time defended his portion of the light heavyweight championship with the frequency of Halley's Comet. The other major circumstance was an event that took place in August 1966. *Sunset* magazine reported it thusly: "Caesars Palace opened on August 5, with 680 rooms in 14 stories on 34 acres. The grand opening featured a three-day party that cost $1 million with a guest list of 1,800."

The first big casino fight took place at Caesars Palace in 1978. It pitted Ken Norton against Jimmy Young in a heavyweight elimination contest. From that time on, and throughout the decade of the eighties, the new address of the Mecca of Boxing was Caesars Palace.

TABLE 6.1: SITE OF MOST HEAVYWEIGHT TITLE BOUTS

Site	Number of Title Bouts
Madison Square Garden	21
Yankee Stadium	16
Caesars Palace	11

In the 110 years since Madison Square Garden hosted its first heavyweight championship—John L. Sullivan versus Joe "Tug" Wilson—it had been the site of 21 heavyweight title fights; in just 12 years, Caesars Palace had hosted 11. Perhaps this came about because the sport needed a fresh look, a facelift for television. Possibly, but the bet here is that the reason for the ascendancy of Las Vegas and Caesars Palace is the same one that

Willie Sutton gave when asked why he robbed banks: "Because that's where the money is."

There have been many classic moments at Caesars: the Sugar Ray Leonard–Thomas Hearns "Showdown" in 1981, when the odds proved to be like quicksand, shifting constantly; the Marvelous Marvin Hagler–Thomas Hearns take-no-prisoners war in 1985, when the go-no go line reached four rounds in the late betting; the Salvador Sanchez–Wilfredo Gomez "Battle of the Little Men" in 1981, when partisan betting by the rival Mexican and Puerto Rican rooters turned Caesars Palace into a state of heightened emotion; the Leonard-Hearns encounter in 1989, when the only proposition to pay off was a long shot, 15–1 on a draw.

But perhaps the greatest moment in Caesars Palace boxing history came on the night of April 6, 1987, when Sugar Ray Leonard, who had assayed as many comebacks as Frank Sinatra, made yet another, this one against Marvelous Marvin Hagler, a warrior thought by many to be the greatest hitter since Lizzie Borden. It was said that the only difference between Hagler's opponents and the *Titanic* was that the *Titanic* went down slower. And Leonard, so the reasoning went, was a blown-up welterweight with only one fight in the previous five years.

And so the betting opened with Hagler a 3–1 favorite. Translated into a money line, it was −300 on Hagler, +240 on Leonard.

Here a quick note is in order. Those man-to-man odds quoted in daily newspapers are real only in the same sense that raisins are real fruit—only technically and in a manner of speaking. They are true odds in the sense that it is an expert assessment of the probability of a certain outcome. When you read that a fighter is a 3–1 favorite, man-to-man, you would expect to lay $30 to collect $10 on the favorite or bet $10 to win $30 on the underdog. But, as George Gershwin was wont to say, "it ain't necessarily so."

What is generally overlooked is the fact that the house takes a small cut out of every bet as a commission. This is called "vigorish," or, simply, "vig." In order to bet the favorite you must *lay* odds of 3–1, bet $30 to win $10 (−300 when stated as a money line); conversely, if you cash a bet on the underdog, you will receive only $20 for each $10 you wagered (+200).

Averaging these two bets, this means that the total of $500 bet on this particular fight straddles the odds and gives the real or "true" man-to-man odds of 2½-to-1 ($300 plus $200 divided by 2). In its infinite wisdom, the house does not look for equal amounts on both sides of the bet, but merely an equal ratio of dollars on both sides. (Table 6.2 shows the true odds and the money lines for each regularly quoted man-to-man proposition.)

One man who did not believe that the Hagler-Leonard fight was a mismatch was Lou D'Amico, head of Caesars Palace Sports Book. Early on, Lou decided to make Hagler a 3–1 favorite. He hoped to encourage enough Leonard money to balance his book. Nearing fight time, as the two superstars crisscrossed the country in a promotional barnstorming tour, the action began to heat up. Hagler money flooded in as more and more people became convinced that he would win. But like the little Dutch boy with his finger in the dike, D'Amico held the odds at 3–1. See Table 6.3 for a sample of fight odds from Caesars Palace.

He had a feeling, one favoring Leonard. But his inspiration wasn't one that would stand up to even the vaguest sort of examination. It came from a dream in which he saw the crowd at Caesars' outdoor stadium standing up before the twelfth and final round shouting, "Sugar Ray . . . Sugar Ray. . . ."

When he revealed this revelation to his aides-de-camp, Vinny Magliulo and Richie Baccelieri, telling them that he had a "feeling" that Sugar Ray would win and that he wanted "to have Leonard going for us in this fight," they were incredulous. When they asked why, all he could say was that he'd "had a dream." Unable to marshal an argument against such fuzzy judgment, they had to go along with his.

And that, as far as Caesars Palace was concerned, was more than enough. In fact, when his friend, actor Jack Klugman,

TABLE 6.2: TRANSLATION OF BOXING ODDS FROM PRICE
QUOTED TO MAN-TO-MAN

Favorite (Laying)	Underdog (Getting)	Man-to-Man Odds	True Odds
−120	−120	Even	6–5, pick 'em
−120	even	6–5	11–10
even	+140	7–5	6–5
−160	+120	8–5	7–5
−180	+140	9–5	8–5
−190	+150	19–10	17–10
−200	+180	2–1	19–10
−225	+190	9–4	21–10
−250	+200	5–2	9–4
−300	+200/−225	3–1	2½–1; 2⅝–1
−350	+250	7–2	3–1
−360	+280	18–5	3¼–1
−400	+300	4–1	3½–1
−450	+325	9–2	3¾–1
−500	+400	5–1	4½–1
−600	+400	6–1	5–1
−700	+500	7–1	6–1
−800	+600	8–1	7–1
−900	+600	9–1	7½–1
−1000	+700	10–1	8½–1

Everything is based on $100; therefore, if the man-to-man odds are 2:1, $200 is wagered on the favorite to win $100 and $100 to win $180 on the underdog. Note that the higher the odds, the broader the spread of dollars, the underdog side not being etched in stone (that is, 3–1 can be stated as −300; +220 or −300; +240).

came to him before the bout, he was what D'Amico calls a "wannabe" bettor—he wanted to bet but he had no conviction about either fighter. When Lou told him about his dream, Klugman bought a piece of the dream and bet on Sugar Ray.

The Marvelous Marvin Hagler that Leonard challenged that fall evening was a warrior who had picked up every glove cast at him in the name of challenge: unbeaten in his last 37 fights, undefeated in 11 years, and the universally accepted middleweight champion for the previous eight years. His style was that of a physical loan shark, one who imposed his will on the enemy, almost as if he fought with a "trespassers-will-be-prosecuted" mentality.

TABLE 6.3: SOME SELECTED FIGHT ODDS AT CAESARS

Fighters	Year	Odds	Go–No Go	
Heavyweights				
Larry Holmes–Muhammad Ali	1980	Holmes 4:1	Does go 8	− 140
			Not go	even
Michael Dokes–Evander Holyfield	1989	Holyfield 7:1	Does go 6	− 140
			Not go	even
Cruiserweights				
Evander Holyfield–Carlos DeLeon	1988	Holyfield 6:1	Does go 6	− 160
			Not go	+ 120
Light Heavyweights				
Sugar Ray Leonard–Donny Lalonde	1988	Leonard 4:1	Does go 8	− 160
			Not go	+ 120
Middleweights				
Marvin Hagler–Roberto Duran	1983	Hagler 4:1	Does go 8	− 160
			Not go	+ 120
Marvin Hagler–Tommy Hearns	1985	pick 'em	Does go 6	even
			Not go	− 140
Marvin Hagler–John Mugabi	1988	Hagler 6:1	Does go 6	even
			Not go	− 140
Marvin Hagler–Sugar Ray Leonard	1987	Hagler 3:1	Does go 6	− 160
			Not go	+ 120
Junior Middleweights				
Tommy Hearns–Roberto Duran	1984	Hearns 4:1	Does go 6	− 140
			Not go	even
Mike McCallum–Donald Curry	1987	Curry 3:1	Does go 8	− 140
			Not go	even

The first round opened with Hagler advancing from his corner, teeth bared in that mirthless smile that usually preceded his deeds of violence. There was one difference from the Hagler of old, however. Instead of advancing in his normal southpaw stance, he came out in an orthodox, right-handed attack, almost as if trying to show Ray up. Meanwhile, Leonard, moving as light as a cucumber sandwich in his salad days, peppered the advancing Hagler. Leonard was forcing Hagler to wage the battle on his own, unfamiliar terms. This pattern continued well into round two, with Hagler offering Leonard a target he couldn't refuse and Leonard accommodating him.

In fact, Hagler continued with his right-handed attack long after its ineffectiveness had become apparent to all but Marvelous Marvin himself. It was as unbelievable as finding out that Santa Claus suffered from vertigo. Hagler backers suddenly found that he wasn't quite the dish they had ordered. Meanwhile, Leonard was moving with concentration in his every move, making conscious efforts with unconscious ease. He won the first four rounds, while Hagler remained hopelessly polite, staking out homesteading rights to the center of the ring and little else.

Then, in the fifth round, Hagler cornered Leonard and got in a left to the head, then a hook to the body and a short left to the face. Leonard countered with a left to the head. Hagler got in a good left to Sugar Ray's head and followed with a good right-left combination with 30 seconds to go. Surely this rally by Hagler was not without meaning. It was the same offensive onslaught that had disassembled previous opponents into smaller pieces. He now had Leonard pinned against the ropes and landed a right at the bell.

Staggering back to his corner, woozy from the battering, Leonard thought, "He doesn't even know I'm hurt. He had me and he didn't know it!" And from that moment on, the fight was Sugar Ray's.

Caring nothing for Hagler's reputation, Leonard began to make dust out of conventional wisdom, landing more punches, and taking the points—and the fight—away from Hagler. Even though Hagler forced him to stand and deliver once again in the ninth round, this time it was Leonard who landed the closing punches in the furious give-and-take along the ropes.

By the twelfth round the crowd was roaring "Sugar Ray . . . Sugar Ray . . ." just as D'Amico had seen in his dream. Leonard began waving his fists in the air to exhort the crowd. The crescendo of cheering put steel in Marvelous Marvin's thoroughbred heart, and he, too, began to wave his fist in the air, almost as if he were playing the raging bull to Leonard's masterful toreador act.

As the round wound to a close, the crowd rose as one to cheer

on the two valiant combatants. And Lou D'Amico walked closer
and closer to the ring, almost in a trance, there to find Jack
Klugman and exchange mutually congratulatory hugs.

By the time the decision had been read (Judges Lou Fillipo
and Dave Moretti scoring 115–113, but each for a different
fighter, and Judge Jo Jo Guerra scoring it an improbable 118–
112 for "the winner . . . and new world middleweight champion . . . Sugar Ray Leonard. . . .") there was the overjoyed D'A-
mico standing at center-ring, with his two aides, Vinny and
Richie, mouths agape, watching him on TV in the Sports Book
back room. The dream had come true.

Short of having a dream, however, how would you go about
handicapping such a fight? Just as there are horses for courses,
there are styles for fighters, styles that make fights. Handicapping a boxing match requires only that you consider your potential bet with the eye of a recruiting sergeant. There's nothing
fancy about it—no numbers to crunch, no records to keep, no
deep thinking. It requires only that you know the styles of both
fighters.

Without an appreciation of styles, sometimes the winner of
the fight can seem to be as unexplained as the absence of deer
on the opening day of the deer hunting season. Take the case
of James Douglas, the Tyson "Buster," who was given the pro-
verbial snowball's chance when he entered the ring against the
heavyweight champion in February 1990. Wags on the Strip
joked that Tyson was not taking his opponent lightly enough.
So slim were his chances thought to be, that when the odds
opened at 35–1, only one brave soul made a bet on Douglas.
The price eventually closed at 42–1 (−4200 on Tyson; +3500
on Douglas). But what soon became evident was that the champion had indeed taken his opponent *too* lightly. He had not gone
into the fight in top mental or physical condition. And his previous win, a one-round swat-out of Carl "the Truth" Williams,
had obscured some of the flaws in his style. In an outcome that
shook the faith of most of boxing's faithful, Douglas exposed

the champ's shortcomings on his way to boxing's biggest upset, a tenth-round knockout of the once invincible Tyson.

The student of styles could have seen it coming, for it was the difference in styles that had done it as much as Douglas himself. Mike Tyson's calling card always has been his baseball bat of a left; he would just lower his shoulder and let it fly. What Buster Douglas did to counter this was simplicity itself: every time the five-foot-nine Tyson set up to let fly, the six-foot-four Douglas would take a half step backward, taking him out of Tyson's range, while the shorter man remained in his range. There Douglas would double jab him, catching him repeatedly. By midfight the champion's right eye was closed, all the better for Douglas to hit him again. And again.

TABLE 6.4: BIGGEST UPSETS IN BOXING HISTORY

James "Buster" Douglas over Mike Tyson	42–1
10th-round KO, February 10, 1990, Tokyo, Japan	
James J. Braddock over Max Baer	10–1
15-round decision, June 13, 1935, Long Island, NY	
Max Schmeling over Joe Louis	8–1
12th-round KO, June 19, 1936, New York, NY	
Cassius Clay over Sonny Liston	7–1
12th-round TKO, February 25, 1964, Miami, FL	
Muhammad Ali over George Foreman	6–1
8th-round KO, October 30, 1974, Kinshasa, Zaire	
Leon Spinks over Muhammad Ali	6–1
15-round decision, February 18, 1978, Las Vegas, NV	
James J. Corbett over John L. Sullivan	4–1
21st-round KO, September 7, 1892, New Orleans, LA	

It always has been a matter of styles. Thomas Hearns has always had the style to give Ray Leonard problems. Granted that Leonard overcame that style in a classic comeback in their first fight; but one must remember that Ray was a natural welterweight that night back in September 1981, while Hearns— whose body gave him the look of a man who had a job in an olive factory dragging through the pimento, was anything but a natural welterweight. When they met again eight years later, Hearns was by now a natural super middleweight, some twenty-plus pounds heavier, and Leonard was but a bulked-up welterweight fighting at super middleweight. The result this time around was different. Hearns floored Leonard twice, although Leonard, by some failed scoring, came away with a draw, one he did not think he deserved.

Incidentally, a draw or a "push" is a very serious business for the house, because it must refund all bets except those made specifically on a draw. In the case of the Leonard-Hearns bout, the odds on a draw were 15–1.

The judges were perhaps unconsciously following another factor the alert bettor must be aware of: return bouts usually follow the form shown in the first fight. Take one of the greatest upsets of all time, the Henry Armstrong–Fritzie Zivic fight in 1940. Armstrong had, at one time, held titles in three separate weight classes; he had lost only once in his previous 60 fights; and he had successfully defended his welterweight title 19 times. Facing him was Zivic, a glorified club fighter with 24 losses on the debit side of his ledger. Armstrong was 4–1 going into the fight, but that night Zivic roughed him up and won the title in a 15-round decision. They immediately were matched for a return bout, and the form held—Armstrong was once again the favorite, albeit at 9–5 this time around. And once again the result was the same: Zivic stopped the "Hurricane," although it only took 12 rounds this time.

TABLE 6.5: THE ODDS AGAINST THE CHALLENGER WINNING A WORLD TITLE BOUT

Class	Odds
Heavyweight	4–1
Light Heavyweight	5–1
Middleweight	4–3
Welterweight	2–1
Lightweight	2–1
Featherweight	3–1
Bantamweight	12–7
Flyweight	4–3

SOURCE: *The World Book of Odds.*

TABLE 6.6: ODDS ON A WORLD CHAMPIONSHIP MATCH
ENDING IN A KNOCKOUT

Class	Odds
Heavyweight	3–1 in favor
Light Heavyweight	4–3 against
Middleweight	7–5 against
Welterweight	4–3 against
Lightweight	even
Featherweight	5–4 against
Bantamweight	2–1 against
Flyweight	5–3 against

SOURCE: *The World Book of Odds.*

TABLE 6.7: ODDS ON A WORLD TITLE BOUT ENDING BY THE
1ST, 5TH, OR 10TH ROUND

Class	1st Round	5th Round	10th Round
Heavyweight	13–1 against	2–1 against	3–2 in favor
Light Heavyweight	40–1 against	3–1 against	3–2 against
Middleweight	41–1 against	5–1 against	2–1 against
Welterweight	28–1 against	7–2 against	2–1 against
Lightweight	35–1 against	5–1 against	2–1 against
Featherweight	62–1 against	16–3 against	2–1 against
Bantamweight	41–1 against	7–1 against	14–5 against
Flyweight	17–1 against	5–1 against	13–5 against

SOURCE: *The World Book of Odds.*

Oh, sure, there have been reversals of form, as witnessed by the second Willie Pep–Sandy Saddler fight, the second Rocky Graziano–Tony Zale fight, and Floyd Patterson and Ingemar Johannson's second and third fights—although it can be argued that the real reversal of form in that series of fights was the first one. Ninety percent of the time, however, the winner of the first bout will win the rematch. To paraphrase Damon Runyon, "the battle is not always to the winner of the last one, but that's the way to bet."

Remember, the name of the game is "styles." That is what makes boxing—and should make your bet for you. But before you jump to conclusions, you should factor in such things as past performances, common opponents, and, last but hardly least, the psychological makeup of the individual fighters.

There are two other betting considerations in boxing. One, despite what you've heard about professionals coming back the next day no matter what happened the day before, boxing is one of the sports in which the bettor *cannot* come back the next day, there not being a big fight each and every day. This is the one element responsible for boxing being a much less important betting sport than football, basketball, or baseball. There is no chance to play catch-up. As one who lost on the Hagler-Leonard fight summed it up, "Waiting for another big fight to get even is like keeping the porch light on for Jimmy Hoffa."

The other consideration is that, as in all sports, money on the favorite tends to come in early, driving the price up. Therefore, if you intend to bet the favorite, try to do so before the effect of public interest can push it down. Conversely, if you favor the underdog, in most cases you will be rewarded by waiting so that you can improve your price.

One last interesting point: In days of yore, the sport of boxing not only was rumored to be but was, in fact, subject to what the first boxing journalist, Pierce Egan, called the "X," meaning the "fix." Over the years, the "X" was part and parcel of the baggage boxing carried with it, with fighters like Joe Gans, Jake LaMotta, and others succumbing to the siren's call of money or other promises to "go into the tank" or "take a dive." But in these days of megabuck fights, there is simply not enough money around to fix a big fight. This alone militates against shenanigans, because the fixers would have to bet millions more just to make their money back and the influx of so much into the betting pool would be enough to flag the fight and take it off the boards. So cynics beware. Although it has happened in the past, like the Black Sox scandal, it's an oddity that now belongs in those while-you-get-your-hair-cut weeklies. You may bet the fights confident that the outcome will be an honest one.

Today, while the interest in two of America's favorite pastimes, boxing and gambling, couldn't be higher, betting on boxing is somewhat limited, owing to the fact that big punters cannot get even quickly after a loss, as they can in football, basketball, baseball, and other sports.

Nevertheless, there is action aplenty. And occasionally a long shot will come home to make it all worthwhile, just as James "Buster" Douglas did in February of 1990 when he beat Mike Tyson in Tokyo at 42–1 odds.

To enjoy the action in the betting arena, all that is needed is an appreciation of the sport, an ability to assess the combatants, and an understanding of the man-to-man and money odds—and maybe a dream or two.

◆ SEVEN ◆

MONEY MANAGEMENT

A few years back, the Internal Revenue Service office in Denver received a call from a man who asked, "How much tax is due on $75,000?" About $41,180, not counting deductions, the caller was told. "Well, how 'bout $150,000?" the caller asked. The bill jumped to $101,980. "Thanks for your help," said the caller. "I'm just deciding whether to buy one or two tickets in the Irish Sweepstakes."

Call it what you will, that is the essence of Money Management—knowing that when fortune comes your way, it usually comes with some strings attached.

Many bettors, even those who refuse to drink water without a strategem, lose sight of the fact that being a winner is a transitory condition, subject to cancellation without further notice. And to bet without a strategy to maximize the winnings is to operate without a safety net.

Just picking winners is not the answer. Almost anyone should be able to pick more winners than losers, even if they're using a dart board. There is no such thing as a 50/50 proposition. When you're bucking 11/10 odds you must win 11 out of 21 bets just to break even. That translates into a 52.38 percent winning percentage.

So a winner is a winner only in a manner of speaking—only if he makes money. To put it another way, a bettor who picks a lot of winners and fails to make money is just another loser.

This shocking fact is ofttimes lost sight of in contemplation of the strategic advantages of betting on a team. And yet it is the very heart of betting. To bet without an eye to profit is worse than a blunder, it's a crime against your pocketbook. And, if you don't know what money management is then you're in the same boat as the writer who once asked Louis Armstrong what "rhythm" was. "Man," Armstrong replied, "if you gotta ask, you'll never know."

A similar story involves the great Wall Street operator J. Pierpont Morgan. Legend has it that a young financier, still wet behind the ears but flushed with the arrogance that youthful success brings with it, once approached Morgan. He said he was interested in buying Morgan's yacht and inquired about the price. "If you have to ask," said Morgan, "then you can't afford it."

Although amusing, the story is misleading, for it is doubtful that Morgan himself ever bought anything without knowing its exact price. After all, he had bought the yacht with money made the old-fashioned way: he'd earned it. He bought low and sold high; he leveraged the market; he got value for his money.

In fact, all of Morgan's financial research and analysis was directed toward one end: to properly evaluate the current and future worth of a share of stock or a piece of property. He didn't care much whether U.S. Steel was better managed or had better manufacturing personnel than Jones & Loughlin; if J. & L. was undervalued he could buy it and make money on the deal. To put it another way, he might handicap J. & L. as a three-point underdog when the line was six and a half.

This is relevant to sports betting because The Caesars Sports Book is really a near cousin to stock markets and commodity exchanges. They are all organized along similar lines and even bear striking physical resemblances to one another, from the big electronic message boards that post prices, futures, and odds to the way business is conducted. To further the comparison, specialists set prices and make markets on the stock market; linemakers determine the odds and adjust the lines to reflect the action in the sports books. They all offer a variety of propositions to invest money in, with the hope of realizing financial gain. Would-be J. P. Morgans in the financial markets would do well to emulate him and seek the right price; so, too, would bettors in Vegas.

However well it may be understood on Wall Street, the notion of *right price* is the least understood concept in sports betting— and the one most essential to success. Although many bettors will tell you they know the meaning of the word *overlay*, in practice it may as well be written in Bulgarian.

When Amarillo Slim, the J. P. Morgan of big-time Vegas gamblers, sent a courier north to Reno to secure an additional point on Denver in Super Bowl XXIV, he did so because all of his years of experience, from his high school days betting football in Texas to high stakes days playing poker in Vegas, had taught him that an extra point in the spread was like money in the bank. Also, like J. P. Morgan, once he had formed his own opinion of the relative merits of the management and personnel of the two teams, he was interested only in how that opinion differed from the price. He bet big because that difference was big.

Although Slim lost the bet, he has never flinched in his conviction that it was a good bet because he knows that that kind of move will be right often enough to be quite profitable. I wouldn't recommend the same bet, but it certainly couldn't hurt to learn a thing or two from Amarillo Slim.

First of all, he bets not as a fan, but as a businessman. The New York City Off-Track Betting Corporation has long had a catchy slogan: "Bet with Your Head, Not over It." It has used it for years not because it is clever, which it is, but because it is good advice. I have a friend, a New Yorker who is an avid fan of the football Giants. He absolutely refuses to bet on them. "If I'm going to make a bet on anything," he explains, "I want to win it. I can't afford to have my judgment muddled by my fandom." He already believes that the Giants can beat any team; it's only a short step to believing that they can beat any line. "When you come right down to it," he continues, "I only care if the Giants win. If they lose, it doesn't mean a thing to me if they beat the spread; if they win, I don't want my joy to be clouded because they failed to cover."

Like the Dow-Jones Index, the Las Vegas line is a dynamic number that moves in the direction of the action it receives. Amarillo Slim didn't just make his bet and retire to the sidelines; he watched closely as it adjusted to the money coming in. It works like an auction. There was more action on the 49ers than the Broncos in Vegas, so the point spread moved upward. There was even more San Francisco money in neighboring Reno, which caused an even bigger bulge in the spread. Sensing a soft spot, Slim took advantage of it.

The general rule for football is: bet early on the favorite, bet late on the underdog. The experienced bettor who wants to bet the favorite gets his money down the moment the windows open. He knows that, just as in the financial markets, a kind of herd instinct governs the actions of the bridge jumpers, those who fancy the fortunes of the favorites. They flock to the windows eager to get their money down. Successive waves push the spread up and the odds down; the bigger the event, the more dramatic the moves. For this reason, the experienced bettor backing the underdog waits to get the best price at the end of the auction.

The experienced bettor also understands long-term probabilities. Amarillo Slim won't apologize for his bet because he knows that over time this kind of wager will pay off much more often than not. My good friend Arne Lang tells us that the fact is, "if you had laid two-and-a-half and taken three-and-a-half on the same game in every NFL game played over the last 10 years, you would have shown a small profit." This reflects the importance of the kicking game in professional football. Since the introduction of sudden death overtime, which is decided 75 per cent of the time by a field goal, three points has become the most important differential in the sport. As Arne puts it, "The bookies are slower to move off the three than any other number in football."

Arne also believes that, from the oddsmaker's vantage point, pro football is the safest action. His knowledge of the game and its probabilities is voluminous; his expertise at setting the odds and tracking the action is confirmed; his confidence is reflected in the highest betting limits of any sport booked in Vegas. Most important of all, he books more action on the NFL *per game* than he does in any other sport. This is incentive enough to ensure good lines. In short, week in and week out, you won't find many soft spots in the NFL line.

(The accuracy of the line used to be provided by an unlikely band of willing co-conspirators. Aiding and abetting the line-makers in their arcane art, an elite panel made up of some of the more prominent members of Las Vegas's colony of professional gamblers had early access to the line. Each Sunday night during the football season, the oddsmakers allowed them to bet into the line before it was unveiled to the public the following day. Any glaring mistakes were quickly spotted by these eagle eyes and affirmed by their action. After the "wise guys" had taken their best shot, the linemakers adjusted the line before posting it for the public. Now, with the odds published on Sunday night, there is no longer time for the panel's consideration, although this does not make it any less accurate.)

This does not mean that there are no soft spots to be found. After all, the final line is made by the public, and "the public," as Alexander Pope put it, "is a fool." The same New Yorker who refuses to bet on the football Giants often bets on Jets games, sometimes for, usually against. Over the years he has been quite successful, basing his bets on good information and soft spots in the line. "Being right here in the market, you have access to a wealth of good information, provided you know how to read between the lines in the New York media," he says. "And New York teams are usually overbet." For that reason, he adds that he doesn't bet on the New York Mets, "who haven't had a good price since Doc Gooden was a rookie."

The NFL playoffs are really the best place to look for bargains in football betting. At this time of year, folks who never thought of betting on football come out of the woodwork to back their local heroes. Their antics can push the spread in all directions. Of course, the linemakers often know what to anticipate. Big cities like New York, Chicago, and Los Angeles can be depended on to back their teams heavily at the windows; smaller cities like Seattle and Jndianapolis don't generate the kind of action that moves the line much. Even Minnesotans can be counted on to back their teams.

It all culminates in the Super Bowl. This is one of the few sports events all year that attracts all kinds—men and women, boys and girls, fans and nonfans, bettors and nonbettors alike. With holiday hangovers a memory and "Pitchers and Catchers" still in the distant future, the Super Bowl offers a universal excuse for a party. Every office and every neighborhood bar have their pools, and man-to-man betting is fast and furious. People who never bet on anything bet on the Super Bowl with their local bookies, for whom it is make-or-break time. (If the federal government could tax all of this casual, illegal betting, it could wipe out the budget deficit in a couple of years.)

This kind of volume originating in such ill-informed circles usually creates a severe imbalance in the line, such as the one Amarillo Slim sought to take advantage of. And it is ultimately for this reason that I must part company with Slim's reasoning. Long-term probabilities no doubt favor this kind of a bet on a regular-season game, but the Super Bowl is a different animal. Not only is the line often seriously distorted, the game all too often develops into a blow-out: 14 of the 25 games played have been won by more than the 13½ points San Francisco had to cover in Reno, including nine of the last 15.

Although the Super Bowl is not a typical case, the lesson is clear: no matter what your handicapping decisions indicate, *don't bet unless the price is right!*

One of the oldest and most simplistic of money management systems is that propounded by the humorist Kin Hubbard: "The only absolutely safe way to double your money," he wrote, "is to fold it once and put it in your pocket." Tongue in cheek though it might be, that's about as fool-proof a gambling system as you're liable to find.

Conversely, equally simplistic, and as foolish as Hubbard's advice is wise, are the so-called "progressive" systems based on the old Martingale method of roulette betting. These come in as many flavors as Häagen-Dazs ice cream, but at bottom they have one thing in common—they require you to increase, usually double, your bets after losing. To this I'll just echo Ben Franklin: "A fool and his money are soon parted." Such a system is just throwing good money after bad; even a short losing streak can quickly raise the ante to the point where the required bet exceeds the house limit and it will be impossible to recoup your losses. The best advice I can give you if you're on a losing streak is: don't.

What really is required in any good money management program is a method that maximizes the profits and minimizes the losses. In other words, press the bet when you're hot, not when you're not! Double up when you're winning, not when you're losing!

Along these lines, one of the very best systems, at least theoretically, showed up in the unlikeliest of places back in 1956, the *Bell Telephone Journal*. Called "the Kelly Criterion" after its author, engineer John Kelly, it is a formula for determining optimal bet-sizing based on the individual's win-proficiency and the current size of his bankroll. It was given great currency later by Edward O. Thorp in his classic text on blackjack, *Beat the Dealer*.

In his article, Kelly put forth this proposition: you pick up the telephone to make a call and find the line already engaged. Ordinarily you would hang up and try again later, but something catches your ear and you listen in. What intrigues you is a familiar voice, that of your friendly neighborhood bookmaker. As the conversation develops it becomes clear that he is discussing the results of a race already run but not yet announced; the bookie is "past-posting" the race, just like Paul Newman and Robert Redford did in *The Sting*. Knowing the winner, he can rig the odds in his favor.

Of course, you now know the winner as well. With a 100 percent certainty of winning your wager, Kelly asks, how much should you bet? If you said 100 percent of your bankroll, you would be right. That's not too hard to grasp, but that's not the point. Nothing you can bet on—short of Kelly's miracle phone call—is ever a sure thing and that's where his analysis comes in.

He goes on to suggest that you have a bad connection and about 40 percent of the conversation is garbled. When you hang up, you are reasonably certain that you have the winner, about 60 percent certain. Now how much should you bet? Not 60 percent of your bankroll. Kelly's conclusion is about 16 percent.

The Kelly Criterion is a bell-curve gradient, similar to that used by teachers in scoring exams. If you would like to use it for football and basketball, the point spread games, you must track your current winning percentage closely and follow the guidelines in Table 7.1.

TABLE 7.1: KELLY CRITERION BETTING LEVELS
The Equation for Determining Optimal Bet Size

What is proper varies from individual to individual according to his win-proficiency and the current status of his bankroll. Kelly betting is a form of progressive betting that is superior to flat betting in terms of maximizing profits—assuming, of course, that one is capable of picking enough winners to exceed the break-even point. If you are able to know what percentage of winners you will pick, what the odds are and how many plays you will make in a season, then you can calculate your season-ending profit ahead of time.

Thus, if one has an established win-proficiency of 60% at 10/11 odds (91 cents return per $1 of investment), the advantage is 16%, based on the following formula:

$A = W - L/P$ The A stands for Advantage (Bet size)
The W stands for Win percentage
The L stands for Loss Percentage $(100 - W)$
And the P for Payoff (to $1)

At a 16% Advantage (Bet size), the formula now looks like this:

$A = 60 - 40/.91 = .16$

TABLE **7.1** (*cont.*)
And, to optimize his profits, the 60% picker should bet 16% of his bankroll each play. If he bets less than 16%, he will not exploit his full advantage and reap the entirety of his potential earnings.

Other Winning percentages to plug into the Kelly Criterion are as follows:

53%—1.4%
54%—3.5
55%—5.5
56%—7.6
57%—9.7
58%—11.8
59%—13.9
60%—16.0
61%—18.1
62%—20.2
63%—22.3
64%—24.4

At *your* winning percentage, you should now be able to figure out how much of your bankroll to bet on each and every play. Neither a higher nor lower figure can yield a larger return.

Bear in mind that this is a best-bet system; you must bet only one game at a time in order to maximize your winning percentage and accurately calculate your bets. Let's say you like the Giants plus three points playing the Redskins in Washington in a 1:00 P.M. (EST) Sunday game. Your bankroll stands at $1,250 and your win percentage is running at 60 percent, the result of six winning bets out of ten games bet this season. This situation dictates a sixteen percent bet of $200. You also like the 49ers minus four versus the Rams in a later game. You bet the $200 on the Giants and sit back to enjoy the game.

The game turns into a nail-biter, as meetings between these two old rivals often do. The score is tied at halftime and you're winning your bet. In the third quarter the Redskins kick a field goal to take the lead, but the Giants are on the march when the period ends. Your bet is a push, but with the Giants threatening, there's no cause for alarm.

You are, however, beginning to sweat the Niners-Rams game.

It's getting late, and the last quarter of the Giants-Redskins game is just getting under way. The Giant drive stalls and they are forced to kick a field goal. The score is tied and you're back on the winning track, but overtime is beginning to be a distinct possibility. If the game ends in a tie, you surely will miss the Niners-Rams kickoff.

The Redskins begin a march up the field, grinding it out on the ground, three or four yards at a time, using up the clock. That's good. Uh-oh! There's a man down on the field. That's bad. After a long examination by the team physician, he walks off under his own power. That's good. But five minutes have elapsed without any change in the game clock. That's bad.

It's doubly bad because CBS cuts away from the Giants game long enough to show the kickoff in San Francisco. You've missed that game.

Meanwhile, back in the nation's capital, Lawrence Taylor sacks Mark Rypien on third and five at the Giants' 20. The Redskins kick another field goal and go up by three points. You're back in Push Country.

The Giants take the kick off, march straight up the field and score a touchdown. The conversion kick gives them a four-point lead just before the two-minute warning. The Redskins go into their two-minute drill and move the ball well. They must put the ball into the end zone: a field goal is meaningless. With first and goal on the eight, four straight incompletions finish off the game. The Giants win.

You have won your bet. Your bankroll now stands at $1,450 and your winning percentage has improved by four percent (actually 3.63 percent, rounded up). Your next bet—and it's too late for the Niners—should be 24.4 percent of $1,450: $353. Let's see, will it be Atlanta +7 Sunday night in the Astrodome or should you wait for the Raiders on "Monday Night Football"?

That's a handicapping decision and beyond the scope of the Kelly Criterion, but from this example you should be able to appreciate how the mechanism works to maximize the profits while limiting the downside losses. If you had lost the bet on the Giants, it would have reduced *both* your bankroll and your winning percentage. The next bet would have been smaller, automatically protecting your capital.

Of course, you had to pass up the tempting bet on San Francisco, but there was no way you could determine the proper bet on the Niners until the Giants and the Skins were finished playing. This is a benefit, not a drawback, of playing the Kelly system: it forces you to be patient. Play your best bet and don't make your next move until you know the outcome of the current one. When you're facing a probable conflict like the Giants-49ers overlap, you must decide before the first game which one looks like the better bet. Set your priorities and stick to them.

One way to leverage your money is through parlays. Contrary to popular perception, this is one of the best ways to build a relatively small bankroll into a larger one.

One reason they are spurned by so many is the common knowledge that a larger winning percentage is needed to profit from parlays. Indeed, this is true. But common knowledge does not always lead to wisdom. Our own "Wizard of Odds," Arne Lang, points out that 54 winners out of 100 is currently enough to return a profit at the Nevada books. That's less than two percent above breakeven when you're bucking the Book's 11/10 odds! (And if you can't do any better that, you have no business playing.) On the other hand, if you are picking better than 60 percent winners, three-team parlays can lead to handsome profits. The difference is in the 6–1 odds currently offered—a lot better than you'll get from your local bookie or on a parlay card.

Of course, the nay-sayers who pooh-pooh parlays point out that the fair odds are 7–1. That's based on the assumption that the bettor is going to be right half of the time and wrong the other half. But if he wins only 50 percent of his straight bets, he's going to lose money however he bets.

To see how parlays produce profits, let's assume that a handicapper picks 70 percent winners (no one can sustain this pace over long periods, but stick with me for the sake of argument). If he bets 300 games at $100 apiece, he'll win $21,000 (210 times

TABLE 7.2

· PAY OFF ODDS ·

FOOTBALL NFL & COLLEGE

PARLAYS — *(Over the Counter)*

2 TEAMS .... PAYS	13 to 5
3 TEAMS .... PAYS	6 to 1
4 TEAMS .... PAYS	10 to 1
5 TEAMS .... PAYS	20 to 1

In the event of a tie, a two team parlay becomes a straight bet. A tie in a three or more team parlay reduces the parlay to the next lowest betting bracket. Thus, a four team parlay becomes a three team parlay, etc.

TEASERS — *(Over the Counter)*

	6 POINTS	6½ POINTS	7 POINTS
2 TEAMS .... PAYS.......	10 to 11	.... 5 to 6	.... 10 to 13
3 TEAMS .... PAYS	8 to 5	.... 3 to 2	..... 6 to 5
4 TEAMS .... PAYS	5 to 2	.... 2 to 1	..... 9 to 5
5 TEAMS .... PAYS	4 to 1	.... 7 to 2	..... 3 to 1
6 TEAMS .... PAYS	6 to 1	.... 5 to 1	..... 9 to 2

In the event of a tie, a two team teaser constitutes "NO ACTION." (ALL money wagered will be refunded.) A tie in a three or more team teaser reduces the teaser to the next lowest betting bracket. Thus, a three team teaser with a tie becomes a two team teaser, etc.

$100) and lose $9,900 (90 times $110—$100 plus $10 vigorish) for a net win of $11,100. If instead he bets 100 three-team parlays at $100 apiece, he can expect to win $20,580 (34.3 times $600) and lose $6,570 (65.7 times $100) for a net win of $14,010! And one of the most attractive aspects of this was that two-thirds less capital was required.

Does that mean that parlays are always the better bet? Probably not, for two reasons. First, it's rare to find three or four games that are equally good bets at the same time; second, because your bets are coupled, you must win them all to win one, unlike straight betting in which your wins and losses can come in random order. For these reasons it is a good policy to maintain a separate bankroll for parlays. When you find a good parlay opportunity, take advantage of the higher odds and bet proportionately less on the parlay while making your normal bets on the individual games. Table 7.2 gives you the pay off odds on football parlays for example.

Finally, a few sensible rules are necessary to protect your hard-earned dollars:

- Keep your betting capital separate from the rest of your bankroll. There is enough pressure on you in a gambling situation without adding the additional stress of having to make back the rent or the kids' money for college tuition.
- Set yourself realistic goals and stick to them. Let's say you start with $1,000 in your kitty and want to double it. Regardless of what kind of money management strategy you are using, once you reach that goal, draw down your profits and start again with $1,000. Another way to do it is to take out half of it—$500—when you reach the goal and raise the goal to $1,500. This keeps more money in the game. And if you are playing a proportional betting system, such as Kelly, it increases the size of your initial bet.
- Don't get giddy when you get ahead. Don't confuse your money with the house's. Once you've won it, it's yours. Treat it with as much respect as you would your last nickel.
- Conduct your betting operations the way you would a business: make sure you are properly capitalized and that *the price is right!*

Finally, remember that in gambling, patience is much more than a virtue, it's a necessity. Racetrackers have a phrase for it—they say a jockey is "sitting chilly" when he keeps his horse reined in on the rail, patiently waiting for a hole to open that he can send his mount through to challenge the leader. Only the very best jockeys have the nerve for it. And they are the big winners.

That's what you have to do to be a winner. Be ready to wait, sitting chilly until the situation is exactly right. As a character in one of William Murray's fine Shifty Anderson racetrack mysteries says, "To be successful at the track, you need an iron ass."

♦ GLOSSARY ♦

action: Any wager; also, the total amount bet, either from the bettor's point of view or that of the house.

added money: In horse racing, additional purse monies in a stakes race contributed by track management over and above entry fees.

also ran: A horse that ran out of the money.

ATS: Against the spread—taking the points—as opposed to betting with the spread and laying the points.

bet: Any wager.

book: A betting establishment that sets odds and accepts wagers on the outcome of sporting events.

bookmaker: A book.

chalk: The favorite.

circled game: A game in which the sports book reduces its normal betting limit.

cover: When the favorite wins by more than the required number of points.

daily double: A horse racing parlay designated by the house, with the odds set by a parimutuel pool. Historically the first two races on the card, recently many tracks have opted to schedule more than one double, the second being on later races. At Caesars the house limits double payoffs to 50:1 except at those tracks in which the house participates in the parimutuel pool.

daily triple: The newest form of exotic bet in which the bettor must identify the winners of three consecutive races, as in a daily double; the races are designated by the track, usually the sixth, seventh, and eighth races.

dime: A thousand dollars.

dime line: A money line in which the vigorish amounts to 10 percent.

'dog: The underdog.

dollar: One hundred dollars.

edge: Advantage.

even money: Even odds.

even odds: Any 50/50 proposition.

exacta: An exotic bet in horse racing. In order to win it, the bettor must successfully identify the horses that finish one-two in a race.

exotic bet: Any bet other than a straight bet—parlays, teasers, quinellas, exactas, trifectas, and so on.

favorite: The entry expected to win an event. The quoted odds reflect the extent to which the choice is favored.

figures: Statistics (see *handicapping*). In horse racing, "figures" usually refers to "speed figures," or "figs."

furlong: An eighth of a mile.

futures: Bets accepted well in advance (usually months) of an event. Caesars maintains futures books on most major events, including the World Series, the Super Bowl, and the Kentucky Derby.

Gold Sheet: A reliable and successful handicapping publication featuring power ratings for football, basketball, and hockey.

handicap: In horse racing, the weight assigned to an entrant in order to equalize the various abilities of all entered.

handicapper: One who studies odds and wagers on the outcome of races or sporting events; at the racetrack, the individual responsible for assigning weights in a handicap race.

handicapping: The art or science of predicting the outcome of sporting events.

hedging: Betting the opposite team or side of your original wager in order to either try to "middle" the game or to reduce the size of the original wager.

home cookin': Colloquial term for home-field (court/ice) advantage.

hook: A half point.

house quinella: A horse racing bet available in sports books in which the payoff is determined by a standard formula (Win Payoff × Half Place Payoff). See *Quinella*

in the money: A horse that finished first, second, or third.

Kelly Criterion: Popular money management scheme for maximizing the profits.

laying the points: Betting the favorite by giving up points.

laying the price: Betting the favorite by laying money odds.

limit: The maximum wager accepted by the sports book.

line: The current odds and/or point spread on a particular event.

linemaker (oddsmaker): The person or persons responsible for establishing the probability of one team defeating another and quoting that in the form of odds and/or points.

lock: The mythical "can't-lose" wager.

long shot: A team, horse, or wager that is unlikely to win.

maiden: A horse that has not won a race.

middle: When both sides of a point spread proposition win.

money line: Odds expressed in terms of money. If a baseball game is quoted as "Dodgers −140 versus Braves +130," Dodger bettors must bet (lay) $140 to win $100 and the backers of the underdog Braves will win $130 for every $100 bet.

morning line: In horse racing, the odds quoted by the track handicapper on each entry before any betting takes place.

moving up (down) in class: A horse that is entered in better (weaker) company than its customary level.

nickel: Five hundred dollars.

nickel line: A money line in which the vigorish amounts to 5 percent.

numbers: See *figures*

odds: The probability of a particular outcome.

oddsmaker: See *linemaker*

odds-on favorite: A horse so favored by the public that the odds are less than even (1–1).

off-the-board: A game in which the sports book is not accepting wagers.

overlay: An advantageous situation for the bettor in which the price on a given wager is greater than the real probability of its success.

over/under: See *totals betting*

parimutuel: Betting pools in which the odds are determined by the proportionate amounts bet on the individual entries.

parlay: A combination wager in which the bettor connects two or more bets and collects odds if successful.

parlay card: A betting novelty popular around the country in which the bettor wagers parlays; not a good bet, as the payoff odds are significantly lower than the true probability.

PC: Percentage.

perfecta: See *exacta*

pick 'em: The game is a tossup; neither team is favored.

point spread: The predicted scoring differential between two opponents quoted by a sports book; favored by most bettors over odds betting in contests in which the probable straight-up outcome makes betting unattractive.

pool: See *parimutuel*

post time: The scheduled time for a particular race to be run. It is illegal in Nevada for a race book to accept wagers after the announced post time in televised races or after two minutes before post time in non-televised races.

power rating: A handicapping tool usually employed in sports in which the betting is against a point spread; the handicapper either makes his own power ratings or uses those in the *Gold Sheet* and similar publications.

price: The line.

prop: See *proposition bet*

proposition bet: A wager offered by the book on a particular aspect of a contest, such as the total score (see "The Super Bowl" chapter).

push: A tie in the betting.

quinella: An exotic bet on two horses to finish one-two in either order; unlike an exacta, it is not necessary to predict the exact order of finish. (See *exacta, house quinella*)

round-robin: A method of parlaying two or more teams or horses in all possible two-team (horse) parlay combinations. For example, a three-team (horse) round-robin of ABC can produce three separate two-team (horse) parlays—AB, AC, and BC.

route: A longer horse race, usually of a mile or more.

runner: A messenger sent to place a bet or collect the winnings.

score: To win a lot of money.

scratch: To remove a horse from a race.

side: When one side of a betting proposition wins and the opposite side ties.

spread: See *point spread*

sprint: A short race, usually less than a mile.

straight-up win: A victory by a point spread underdog.

taken down: A horse that was disqualified and placed in a lower finishing position.

taking the points: Betting the underdog with its advantage in the point spread.

taking the price: Betting the underdog and accepting money odds.

ten-cent line: See *dime line*

totals bet: A proposition bet in which the bettor speculates that the total score by both teams in a game will be more or less than the line posted by the sports book.

tout: A familiar figure at the racetrack—and, to a lesser degree, at the sports books, as he is not tolerated—the tout will "give you a winner" if you let him. But don't.

tout services: Modern marketing's answer to the traditional tout, these services will offer you all kinds of "mortal locks." Ignore them. See also *lock, tout*

tout sheet: Publications that make predictions on the outcome of sporting events; generally used derisively, the term nevertheless encompasses the whole field, including such reliable publications as the *Green Sheet* and the *Gold Sheet.*

trifecta: A wager on three horses to finish first, second, and third in exact order in the same race.

true odds: The real probability of any outcome happening, expressed in odds.

underdog: In team games, the favorite's opponent.

underlay: A disadvantageous situation for the bettor in which the price on a given wager is lower than the real probability of its success.

vigorish: The commission extracted by the book for accepting the bet; usually 10 percent, it varies according to the bet and the book. See *dime line, nickel line*

wager: Any bet.

wheel (key): In horse racing, a strategy for exotic wagering in which a key horse is combined with many or all other entries in the field; also used in sports parlays and teasers.

winter book: See *futures betting*

wise guy: A sophisticated, well-informed handicapper.

writer: The person designated by the race and sports book to accept bets from the public.

◆ SUGGESTED READING/ BIBLIOGRAPHY ◆

Basketball Handicapping, by Mike Lee, Las Vegas, Nevada: GBC Press, 1979.

This 1979 technical paper (16 pages) is today still the best buy anywhere if you want to learn how to establish and modify power ratings (pro and college); understanding home court versus road factor and analyzing the streak factor.

Basketball: Picking Winners Against the Spread, by A. J. Friedman, Las Vegas, Nevada: GBC Press, 1978.

Excellent for beginners who want to know the basics, including sports services and how they function; how to keep proper records; understanding power ratings; betting totals (overs-unders); parlays; teasers. 64 pages.

Beating the Bookie, by Huey Mahl, Las Vegas, Nevada: GBC Press, 1975.

The first important book on sports betting published by Gambler's Book Club in Las Vegas. Mahl, still one of the most innovative and respected names in the writing and betting business, focuses on football betting (including football pools and 100 squares); baseball (understanding the line, overs and unders and parlay cards); and touches on basketball, hockey, and boxing betting. 64 pages.

Betting the Bases, by Mike Lee, San Clemente, California: self-published, 1981.

Purely on baseball betting, by one of the sharpest young handicappers of the past two decades. Discusses key factors like peaking, streaking, favorites, sweep game fallacy, how layoffs affect pitchers. 70 pages.

Book on Bookmaking, by Ferde Rombola, Glendale, California: Romford Press, 1984.
Fascinating comparisons between legalized sports betting and horse racing vs. illegal variety. Covers baseball, football, basketball. Ideas, advice, anecdotes about bookmakers, their customers, and the search for the "informational edge." 148 pages.

Castaways $100,000 Pro Football Championships, by Martin Mendelsohn, Las Vegas, Nevada: GBC Press, 1980.
Week-by-week strategies, angles, methods of handicapping from dozens of top handicappers and sports services vying for $65,000 first prize in the grandaddy of all football handicapping contests during the 1979 season. The author picked the brains of most entrants to find out how and why they bet on what pro teams and how they finally wound up in the standings after betting 224 regular season battles. 64 pages.

Education of a Sports Bettor, by Bob McCune, Las Vegas, Nevada: McCune Sports Investments, 1989.
Respected handicapper, bettor McCune discusses how to handicap all major sports, betting lines, keeping records, power ratings, sports service pluses and minuses, money management techniques. 390 pages.

Gambling Times Guide to Basketball Handicapping, by Barbara Nathan, Van Nuys, California: Gambling Times, 1984.
Highly respected lady handicapper gives you the ABCs, fundamentals of handicapping basketball (mostly on pros), from choosing a sports service to handicapping versus the spread and totals; developing your own system; the home court factor. 252 pages.

Handicapper's Pointspread Notebook, Los Angeles, California: Nation-Wide Sports Publications.
Published by the prestigious sports service newsletter *The Gold Sheet* (owned by Mort Olshan), this annual publication gives bettor 14 years of college and pro scores, spreads for football. Also includes pro totals for three years. Good basic data base for back-checking trends, angles for handicapping theorists. 120 pages.

How to Beat the Bookies at Pro Football, by Allan Sandler, Miami, Florida: 1974.
One of the first purely-on-football betting books, still has sharp, incisive

advice to offer on handicapping, including line adjustments, impact of player injuries and money management. Imparts solid advice on how to bet at various points in the season when teams are still competing for playoff berths or are eliminated. Special supplement in book focuses on the bettor's dream situation, better known as "middling." 148 pages.

Professional Computer Handicapping System: Football, by Bob Clare, Las Vegas, Nevada: R-Way Sportsware, 1990.

One of the first and best methods of programming your IBM-compatible computer to handicap professional football. Takes you step by step through the programming process. Author offers free phone support (but call is on you). 60 pages.

Race and Sports Book Management, by Michael Roxborough and Mike Rhoden, Las Vegas, Nevada: Las Vegas Sports Consultants, Inc.

Breakthrough manual teaches the novice to the sports or race book industry in Nevada how to understand the linemaking process, how to book all sports—baseball, football, basketball, hockey, boxing, parlay cards, futures. Explains timing in "hanging the line," importance of clear house rules, proper phone account procedure. Should help the bettor to understand how the house operates. Small section (15 pages) focuses on race book operations. Perfect reference for those who want a career in the industry or understanding how the industry operates, legally. 128 pages.

Any book listed above may be ordered from Gambler's Book Shop, also known as GBC Press, via toll-free number outside Nevada at 1-800-634-6243 (9–5 LV time, Mon. to Sat.) or write GBC for a free catalog at 630 South 11th St., Las Vegas, Nevada 89101.